ABDUL QUAYYUM KHAN KUNDI

Thoughts: God, Science, and Human Nature

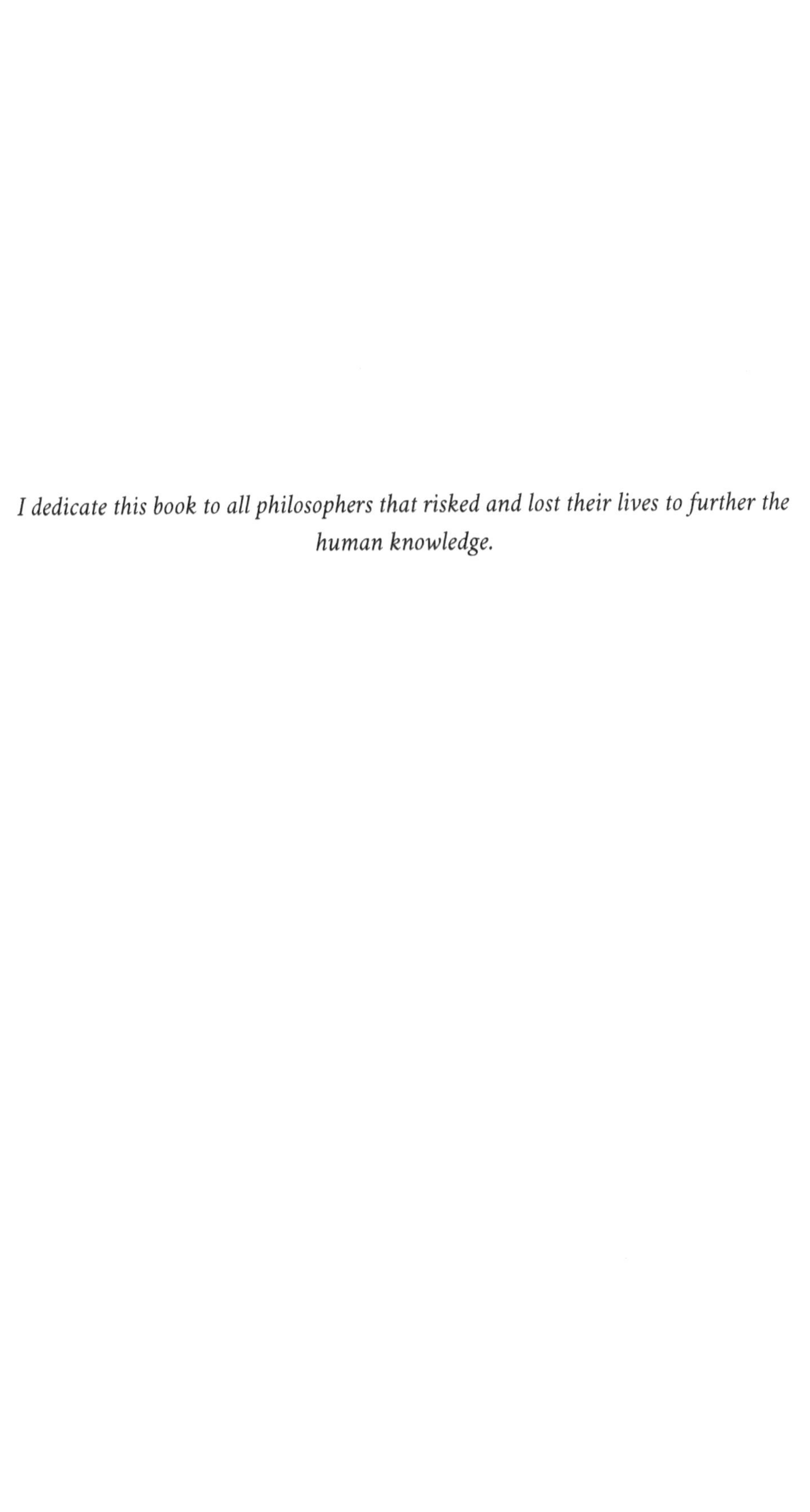

I dedicate this book to all philosophers that risked and lost their lives to further the human knowledge.

Contents

Acknowledgement

My journey of exploration owes its existence to the unwavering support and inspiration from a network of friends, family, and mentors. Each of them has left an indelible mark, offering guidance, posing thought-provoking questions, and challenging me to push the boundaries of my intellectual capacity. The impact spans a diverse spectrum, from the guiding hand of my primary school teacher to the wisdom imparted by mentors of the present day. It's a collective effort that has crafted my path, and it's impossible to measure the immeasurable value each has contributed to my growth.

Preface

When I sat down to start writing this book about random thoughts on God, science, and human nature, the question I had was: What value does it offer to the reader? It was a difficult question to tackle because the thoughts I am going to present are not definitive answers to many of the puzzling riddles about the universe and our place in it. The sole purpose of this book is to try providing a new perspective that might enable you to look at the world differently. If any of these ideas help you to think differently or help you to develop new insights, then the purpose would be served.

Philosophers maintain a degree of skepticism and tend to question the status quo. It does require some degree of brevity as a multitude of people are not comfortable in changing their ways. Socrates learned it the hard way when he was condemned to death by a citizen jury. He was punished for endangering the peace of the community and polluting the thoughts of the youth. Socrates was not the only one many other philosophers had to endure hardships for their thoughts and ideas.

Philosophy deals with questions that are not satisfactorily answered by the existing knowledge at a given time. The Greek philosopher Socrates asked probing questions at a public square to demonstrate that maintaining a degree of skepticism is critical to continue exploring a thought to understand it better. Similarly, Bertrand Russell, a philosopher of the modern era, advises maintaining certain doubts about metaphysical speculations but considers it an important activity to further knowledge. Rene Descartes raised concerns about the reality of existence and questioned whether it exists in the mind.

Classical English writer Shakespeare presented seven stages a person goes through in a lifetime. Starting from infancy, moving towards childhood, becoming a youth, then a soldier to defend ideals, arriving at middle age, becoming a mentor to the next generation, and finally a dotard ready to exit from the world stage. Intellectually a person goes through four stages of his life. The first stage is a learner to develop faculties, to prepare to play a role in society as an adult. The second stage is a craftsman to produce for the community under supervision. The third stage is to become a supervisor for the next generation. The fourth and last stage is that of a mentor or a sage sharing his wisdom and knowledge rather than being physically active.

From whichever perspective we look at, childhood is a period when a person is at the height of his creative instinct because there is no inhibition with concerns about the reaction of others to outlandish ideas. A child is fearless, or some would say shameless, in his presentation of a thought that is new to him. A probable reason for this attitude could be that in childhood we have a vague idea of self that means the ego is still dormant and has not awakened to the possibility of its place in the world. Awareness of self creates anxieties about being accepted by others and avoiding rejection. A philosopher has to maintain that childlike fearlessness in exploring and explaining the secrets of life and reality. While aware of his own identity and place in a community, a philosopher cannot allow society to dictate terms of association to contain the flight of his thought. In this endeavor, he cannot be sure that whatever he explores will be proven correct, but he is honest about expressing and presenting it to the world. He has to allow the world to expound on it in whichever manner they deem fit. The tools at the disposal of an explorer are knowledge that is already presented by other philosophers. A mind to contemplate this knowledge, and the power of intuition to arrive at new findings that have hitherto remained unexplored. It is like an artist using paint and a canvass that has been used by other painters millions of times. Every new painting is one more possibility that was not conceived earlier by anyone else.

The book is about metaphysical speculation, the concerns I had in writing this book were, what if I am wrong in my thoughts? Should I withhold this book until I am sure about the ideas presented? In the end, I decided it is better to publish it for two reasons. First, I believe you are intelligent to identify the errors of judgment. Secondly, if perfection is sought and possible in compiling a book on the human condition, from the earliest development of thought, then human knowledge would not have progressed much. Refinement in knowledge has been achieved over centuries by removing the errors in past speculations and discoveries. That process continues. It does not mean that I have not contemplated these ideas as thoroughly as I could before presenting them to you.

One theme that you will find throughout the book is finding a rational basis for theological ideas. Religion is usually associated with the emotional and irrational side of human nature. It is because of the difficulty to prove, scientifically, the existence of God. But does this mean that God is an irrational idea? I do not think so. Eventually, science will, and should confirm the existence of God, although comprehending His true nature and essence may be beyond its capability. It must not ring alarm bells for scientists because there is increasing progress towards the rationalization of social sciences, including politics and economy, using big data and social media platform technologies.

In a similar fashion, we cannot continue allowing religion to remain backward by labeling it as a force of division and intolerance. Religion has been present in the human psyche throughout our existence. Like all other human enterprises, it has its own positive and negative impacts. Instead of working towards an interfaith alliance, which is a new buzz word among social scientists, it may be more beneficial to rationally look at its social and individual values. In other words, through this book, I am trying to make a case for the development of a new discipline of religious sciences. It is different from a theology that deals with a dogma that is an artistic and cultural aspect of the religion. Religious sciences should deal with metaphysical speculations about the existence or non-existence of God, the soul, and the social impact of its moral code. It may not be an easy thing to do because of our emotional association with religion. This barrier is quite substantial and would require consistent effort to overcome. The starting point could be a reformation of religious education imparted to preachers as well as adherents. It is not a suggestion to create some form of a new religion, rather an effort to study the impact of religion on our social, political, and economic lives.

Just 200 years ago, if someone used a smartphone, in a crowded bazaar, the people would be sure the person had supernatural powers. Similarly, no one would have believed that there will be a time when a machine, the airbus A380, will carry 550 people and their luggage through the sky traversing over 8000 miles (about 12874.75 km) without stopping. Material science has made substantial progress because of our extensive focus on it. It has enabled us to improve our standards of living and brought us closer to becoming a global community. When I suggest creating a new discipline, religious sciences, I am proposing that science that has so far focused on the understanding of matter should now give some attention to the metaphysical questions of our spirituality. For instance, instead of accepting uncertain big bang theory, some scientists should explore whether the first creation happened because of the deliberate action of God as an agent. It is at the back of the mind of scientists that inspired them to name various phenomena in terms of God. Higgs Boson that helped us understand how matter exhibits mass was called a God particle. In this quest for God as the first agent, they may not fully answer the nature of God, as it is beyond human comprehension, but prove his existence that started all this. The impact of religion on societies is another area that requires a scientific basis of understanding. Science and religion are not disengaged but reinforce each other. The Quran challenges why don't people ponder over the things around them to find Him. It demands an intellectual journey to God through all our faculties, rather than become a blind follower through a leap of faith that many preachers promote. Classical Greek philosophers presented the metaphysical idea of a first cause to represent God that is not enough to satisfy our rational minds today. The advancement of science is approaching the sophistication to provide the empirical evidence of proving God. It is about time we use all the tools available in the laboratory to explore the spiritual side of our existence that is anchored, with understanding, the idea of God.

Some of the ideas presented in the book were first published as opinion pieces published in various newspapers. The book expands on it and presents it in a more organized fashion. There are two key themes you will find throughout the book. First, that science and religion reinforce rather than negate each other. Second, we may be a superior species, but we have to make efforts to understand the mind and psychology of other species. Our knowledge of animal nature is rudimentary and biased. We treat animals with contempt and consider them inferior. We fail to recognize that our lives, here on earth, will be untenable without these other species. Many challenges and hurdles remain to understand and learn from the animal kingdom. The lack of a working communication medium is one of them. Our knowledge of the universe will remain incomplete until we unlock the wisdom of other species. Humility is not our strongest trait.

It is with this perspective I present this book to you. I believe men and women may have differing muscular strength and psychological makeup but endowed with the same intellectual capabilities. Wherever a muscular term is applied, it is more a matter of speech than gender bias. Verses of the Quran, used throughout the book, are from the translation of Abdullah Yusuf Ali. References to the Bible are from King James Version. One of the difficulties you would experience is the repetition of some terms like consciousness, reality, mind, God, and a priori. It is because other synonyms to convey the same idea is hard to find. Names of Prophets are in Eastern format rather than the West. Names of prophets succeed the salutation in Islamic tradition. Any errors and omissions are regretted and are entirely my responsibility.

Abdul Quayyum Khan Kundi
July 27, 2020

God, Religion & Atheism

God

I am a believer in one God. I arrived at this conclusion after spending considerable time exploring the questions of how this universe came to be? What is the purpose of our lives? Why so much injustice in the world if God exists? Throughout this book, we will explore the question about God. To me, it was clear that there has to be one all-powerful God for this universe to function seamlessly like a clockwork. I will share some of the knowledge that helped in arriving at this conclusion.

Science plays a dominant role in the 21st century. We have made significant progress in using materials to improve our standards of living. But it is still unable to explain the world around us with certainty. Science is at the early stages of its evolution to explain various phenomena about the creation of the universe. It is so far unable to explain where the dense matter came from that exploded in the Big Bang to give rise to this universe. It assumes rather than confirm through various experiments and theories. It relies on unknowns to make these theories workable.

After the universe came to be, the next stage was the evolution of living beings. The theory of evolution fails to explain why humans, that are a later species, in the chronological process of creation, are so advanced in their intellect, expressed in language and arts. While other species that are older in existence still lag far behind. Religion provides an explanation, but science does not.

"Science is cognitively unnatural – it's difficult," says Robert McCauley. He authored the book *Why Religion is natural while Science is not*. He explains his thought, "Religion, on the other hand, is mostly something we don't even have to learn because we already know it." Social scientists agree that there has never been a period in recorded human history that the idea of God was absent from the psyche of a community. Does it mean that God is a necessary condition for normative human existence? There is no definite answer to this question because there has never been a society without some belief in God. God has always been present. Whether it is monotheism or in the Hindu tradition giving shape and form to various attributes of an all-powerful being. Even in societies pursuing communist ideology, that ban the practice of organized religion, people secretly practice prayers and rituals. Communist China does not allow the observance of religious practices and establishing places of worship. To counter that state ban, many secret religious organizations have emerged like Falun Gong.

Science suggests that all living beings are organisms or machines created from a combination of chemical elements present in the universe. It fails to explain how these elements come together to form living species that have varying degrees of consciousness, intellect, and ability to perform a synchronized mechanical movement. Science does not explain the agent that provides these characteristics. Religion comes to the rescue. It calls this agent soul, with a caveat, that it is created by God. In a similar vein, science explains death as a physical phenomenon whereby the machine that functioned as the human body has developed a malfunction and is unable to continue. At the advent of death, it returns the chemical elements to the universe. Since it does not recognize the soul, there is no curiosity about what happens to it when it departs from the body.

Humans have a tendency to verify the idea of God through their rational capacity. It is like collecting sea in a small container. The size of the sea is too big to fit in it. When we fail to achieve that then we try to resolve this paradox by resizing the God to conform to our human limitations and exhibit human tendencies. In other words, a God that has to behave with human instincts and if He fails to harmonize with this mold, then the idea of God has to be rejected altogether. We cannot encompass the full essence of God, but we are reminded of His presence every day in form or the other.

These were the arguments that inspired me to believe in one God. It was paramount to tackle the question of God at the start of the book because we will keep coming back to this theme throughout this discourse. Science will ultimately find God, but until then, it may consider God an irrational concept. Ignoring its limitations, it raises an issue about relying on revealed knowledge to believe in God.

* * *

Atheism and Faith

I am fascinated by the atheist because it seems fantastic that they could reject the idea of God despite the inadequacy of science to explain the physical world around us with certainty. To understand their arguments, I am always eager to meet an atheist with the hope that some new information will be shared to shake the foundation of my faith in one God. But most of the time, I hear the repetition of the same arguments again and again. They suggest that faith has a certain degree of irrationality, although, in the Muslim religious text Quran, God has challenged that those with intellect should ponder over the universe to reaffirm our belief in Him.

Renowned atheist and scientist Richard Dawkins, and his book 'The God Delusion', are much quoted on atheism. I read his book with anticipation that he will use the power of rationality to prove the non-existence of God rather than criticizing the irrationality of believers. I understand that he is disappointed that God does not react to human impulses and, in a world of instant gratification, does not discharge punishments for sins and injustices on the fly or prevent acts of cruelty committed by autocrats and oppressors. He has adopted the logic of the negative affirmation that is to prove that a concept is untrue to deduct that the opposite could be true.

Here is a quote from his book: "An atheist in this sense of philosophical naturalist is somebody who believes there is nothing beyond the natural, physical world, no supernatural creative intelligence lurking behind the observable universe, no soul that outlasts the body and no miracles—except in the sense of natural phenomena that we don't yet understand.". The statement ends with the confession that we do not understand the natural phenomena yet.

The examples quoted by Mr. Dawkins to prove Godless world, for instance, using a hypothesis that a person could believe there is a flying kettle in the cosmos. Suggesting that God is nothing but a figment of the imagination of the believers. Interestingly, his presentation of the scientific examples is almost always succeeded by a suggestion that progress must have been made by the time his book is read, confessing that science is still in an evolutionary stage and a work in progress. Here is another excerpt from the book: "Hard-nosed physicists say that the six knobs were never free to vary in the first place. When we finally reach the long-hoped-for Theory of Everything, we shall see that the six key numbers depend upon each other, or on something else as yet unknown, in ways that we today cannot imagine". He refuses to discuss the origin of the six key numbers on which the existence of universe hinges. He is pinning his hope on the 'Theory of Everything' to replace God, as the originator of the cosmos and life.

I feel sorry for naturalist Mr. Charles Darwin, whose 130 years old theory of evolution, presented in a book titled 'On the Origin of Species', is quite leisurely quoted by atheists, and Mr. Dawkins is no exception. It is important to note that Mr. Darwin never rejected the idea of a Creator that set evolution into motion. He made concerted efforts to correct the impression that he was an atheist. He preferred to be considered an agnostic. He states in the book that "Natural selection has been the main but not the exclusive means of modification". In the same book in the chapter titled 'Organs of extreme Perfection and Compilation' he writes that "To suppose that the eye with all its inimitable contrivances for adjusting the focus to different distances, for admitting different amounts of light, and for the correction of spherical and chromatic aberration, could have been formed by natural selection, seems, I freely confess, absurd in the highest degree". He concludes this thought with these words "When we reflect on these facts, here given much too briefly, with respect to the wide, diversified, and graduated range of structure in the eyes of the lower animals; and when we bear in mind how small the number of all living forms must be in comparison with those which have become extinct, the difficulty ceases to be very great in believing that natural selection may have converted the simple apparatus of an optic nerve, coated with pigment and invested by transparent membrane, into an optical instrument as perfect as is possessed by any member of the articulate class".

Using the theory of evolution as his basis, Mr. Dawkins writes that "We can deal with the unique origin of life by postulating a very large number of planetary opportunities. Once that initial stroke of luck has been granted—and the anthropic principle most decisively grants it to us -natural selection takes over: and natural selection is emphatically not a matter of luck". It is noteworthy that to explain the origin of life on earth, a stroke of statistical luck is employed, but from there on a rational explanation of natural selection that is scientifically justified. The whole book is full of ideas that are based on assumptions to justify negation of God. Despite confessing repeatedly that science has not worked out all the mysteries of the universe, he does not dissuade from rejecting God out rightly or at least delay the verdict until science progresses some more. Referring to the theory of natural selection, he confesses that scientists do not know why birds, or some other species engage in a particular act but is sure the most intellectual of all species humans are wasteful by believing in God. He thinks all other species are economizing in their act of living except the silly human that is wasting time and resources by pursuing a faith and engaging in prayers, sacrifices, fasting, and charity. He is suggesting humans are not as intelligent as they think of themselves since they are not as good an economizer in nature as other species. It is interesting to note that science is still not able to decipher the consciousness of animals and other species. We can't say, with certainty, that they do not prostrate before or believe in God.

Mr. Dawkins selectively assumes that people of faith do not believe in evolution. There is no proof of it especially for Muslims since the Quran presents evolution. He seems to be unaware that the Quran, a religious book, has validated the evolutionary nature of life in the following verses:

Chapter 6 Verse 2: He it is created you from clay, and then decreed a stated term (for you). And there is in His presence another determined term; yet ye doubt within yourselves!

Chapter 7 Verse 54: Your Guardian-Lord is Allah, Who created the heavens and the earth in six days, and is firmly established on the throne (of authority): He draweth the night as a veil o'er the day, each seeking the other in rapid succession: He created the sun, the moon, and the stars, (all) governed by laws under His command. Is it not His to create and to govern? Blessed be Allah, the Cherisher and Sustainer of the worlds!

Chapter 11 Verse 61: To the Thamud People (We sent) Salih, one of their own brethren. He said: "O my people! Worship Allah: ye have no other god but Him. It is He Who hath produced you from the earth and settled you therein: then ask forgiveness of Him, and turn to Him (in repentance): for my Lord is (always) near, ready to answer."

Chapter 21 Verses 30 – 33: Do not the Unbelievers see that the heavens and the earth were joined together (as one unit of creation), before we clove them asunder? We made from water every living thing. Will they not then believe? And We have set on the earth mountains standing firm, lest it should shake with them, and We have made therein broad highways (between mountains) for them to pass through: that they may receive Guidance. And We have made the heavens as a canopy well guarded: yet do they turn away from the Signs which these things (point to)! It is He Who created the Night and the Day, and the sun and the moon: all (the celestial bodies) swim along, each in its rounded course.

Chapter 22 Verse 5: O mankind! if ye have a doubt about the Resurrection, (consider) that We created you out of dust, then out of sperm, then out of a leech-like clot, then out of a morsel of flesh, partly formed and partly unformed, in order that We may manifest (our power) to you; and We cause whom We will to rest in the wombs for an appointed term, then do We bring you out as babes, then (foster you) that ye may reach your age of full strength; and some of you are called to die, and some are sent back to the feeblest old age, so that they know nothing after having known (much), and (further), thou seest the earth barren and lifeless, but when We pour down rain on it, it is stirred (to life), it swells, and it puts forth every kind of beautiful growth (in pairs).

Chapter 32 Verse 4 – 5: It is Allah Who has created the heavens and the earth, and all between them, in six Days, and is firmly established on the Throne (of Authority): ye have none, besides Him, to protect or intercede (for you): will ye not then receive admonition? He rules (all) affairs from the heavens to the earth: in the end will (all affairs) go up to Him, on a Day, the space whereof will be (as) a thousand years of your reckoning.

Chapter 32 Verses 7 – 9: He Who has made everything which He has created most good: He began the creation of man with (nothing more than) clay, And made his progeny from a quintessence of the nature of a fluid despised: But He fashioned him in due proportion, and breathed into him something of His spirit. And He gave you (the faculties of) hearing and sight and feeling (and understanding): little thanks do ye give!

Chapter 41 Verses 9 – 12: Say: Is it that ye deny Him Who created the earth in two Days? And do ye join equals with Him? He is the Lord of (all) the Worlds. He set on the (earth), mountains standing firm, high above it, and bestowed blessings on the earth, and measure therein all things to give them nourishment in due proportion, in four Days, in accordance with (the needs of) those who seek (Sustenance). Moreover He comprehended in His design the sky, and it had been (as) smoke: He said to it and to the earth: "Come ye together, willingly or unwillingly." They said: "We do come (together), in willing obedience." So He completed them as seven firmaments in two Days, and He assigned to each heaven its duty and command. And We adorned the lower heaven with lights, and (provided it) with guard. Such is the Decree of (Him) the Exalted in Might, Full of Knowledge.

When we look at an ant, can we say that it has not fully evolved? Because if it continues on the path of evolution, then it will not be an ant but some other species. Our knowledge of animals is not advanced enough to be sure that ants have faith in a Creator or questions who created them and why? It just performs the functions that have been assigned, without objecting to it. If everything that exists has to have a logical, rational, and predictable behavior then humans have not evolved perfectly as they still have superstitions, emotions, and mysticism that cannot be explained by science. It is this superstitious, emotional, and irrational nature that produces music, literature, and arts. In a similar vein, if this superstitious behavior produced dogma, it cannot be attributed to God.

Another conclusion one can draw from these examples, quoted from Mr. Dawkins's book, is that language, as a human enterprise, has both rational and irrational expressions intrinsic in it. Because if it was truly rational, with no facility for irrationality, then it would be impossible to express illogical thought using it. We will talk in detail about language as a human enterprise later in the book.

Science is hinged upon the predictability of recurring phenomena without fail, for example sun rising/setting every day or an electron revolving tirelessly around a nucleus. A phenomenon that is unique with unpredictable outcomes and non-measurable attributes will naturally fail the test to qualify as a verifiable entity. Since God is beyond predictability it is difficult for science to take the measure of God, and hence their disbelief in Him. In a way, science is a commentary on the physical world around us rather than a creative force that has developed any new laws that were not already present in nature. Using a commentator, science, to reject a creative force is an unbridgeable paradox. It's like an art critic telling Picasso how he should have painted his masterpiece. Quran has made it clear that mankind was aware of the existence of God at the time of original creation in another dimension and will find God through rational contemplation during its tenure on earth. Scientific discovery is one of the many tools that can help in this quest for God.

Using the same approach as Mr. Dawkins's let me throw three scientific challenges at you. I would like you to gather all the scientists to achieve any one of the following three feats. First, create a living thing, even a mono-cell, from nothing. Second, maintain a living thing such that it never ages. Third, create a product that does not decay over time. What have these challenges got to do with the question of the existence of God? Well, if an imaginary kettle flying in the space could be used by Mr. Dawkins to prove there is no God, then at least these challenges can be tried in a lab on earth. His book mentions survey results whereby the majority of scientists overwhelmingly confess to being atheists. No wonder because there is an occupational hazard to believe in an entity not confirmed in a lab and could subject a person to ridicule among his peers. Mr. Dawkins, like many others before and after him, has equated believing in dogma as equivalent to believing in God when these are two independent actions and not mutually inclusive.

Humans are complex creatures having both rational and irrational attitudes intrinsic to their nature, or they would not have emotions. These emotions, like love, hate, or envy, cannot be explained rationally but exhibit an irrational aspect of human consciousness. It is not possible to separate these two conflicting attitudes as it co-exists as part of human nature. I do not know any scientist that is devoid of emotions. The day they achieve complete rationality of self will be a big leap forward to settle the question of God. Superstition is a heightened state of the irrational part of the human psyche that is blamed by atheists to be the prime mover for believing in the existence of God. The picture of heaven presented in the Quran is such that there will be no feelings of envy, jealousy, or longing as these emotions will have no utility.

Chapter 11 Verse 108: *And those who are blessed shall be in the Garden: They will dwell therein for all the time that theheavens and the earth endure, except as thy Lord willeth: a gift without break.*

In that heavenly state, God will be an unquestioned phenomenon.

God conveys to us that an intellectual or rational self needs assistance to recognize Him. To help us in this quest, God revealed books. He designated Prophets to convey these divine revelations. Unfortunately, all those original texts are lost, except the Quran. Islam wanted to reduce the reliance on irrational and appealed to the rational side of men. It was probably for this reason, in verses of the Quran, God has challenged us to ponder over the physical world. Unlike past prophets, the messenger of Islam, Prophet Mohammad (PBUH) did not demonstrate any supernatural powers to exhibit miracles even though conservative Muslims consider the book itself to be a miracle.

The challenge is to recognize God using a balanced approach between rational and irrational consciousness. The combination of these two is unique to each person, depending on their life experiences. Those that rely too much on rationality have a chance to make a wrong judgment conversely that use the irrational self also tend to overplay their hand and commit excesses displeasing the very God they want to please.

I agree with atheists that the followers of faith can commit excesses. These violators should know that God has warned these people, in the Quran, not to associate lies with His message. My understanding of atheists' arguments is that they have a utilitarian conception of God. In this view, since the universe can supposedly function on autopilot, hence it proves the nonexistence of God. They also expect God to intervene to prevent wars and eradicate human suffering. Mr. Dawkins has spent considerable ink and paper to talk about abuses committed by people of faith. What I fail to understand is how these human atrocities can be associated with God. His focus is to reject the existence of God rather than highlight acts of people in the name of God. He feels that religion has failed society by instigating wars and conflicts. If China, as a communist country, can be considered as an atheist majority country, then the evidence does not suggest they are any different. In the West, we do have a political equivalent of an atheist in the form of secular governments. Wars in Afghanistan, Libya, Iraq, Syria, Ukraine, and Vietnam, for example, demonstrates that the secular governments are as deadly as a theocracy.

The majority of atheists have an emotional argument against God. They cannot reconcile the existence of a God and the wars, illnesses, and injustices of life. In their view, the presence of God should have guaranteed the elimination of these trials and tribulations. But in almost all revealed books, God never promised that this life would be easy. In these scriptures, God informed us that life, on earth, will be challenging. Those that go through it, with an upright character, are rewarded in another dimension.

* * *

Nature and Human Existence

British philosopher Bertrand Russell recorded two interviews in the 1950s talking about faith and the human condition. One aired by British Broadcasting Corporation (BBC), and the other was a discussion with Alan Watts (links provided in the reference section at the end of the book). It was interesting to hear him speak about the human condition with an emphasis on defining human life, religion, and the destructive force of fanaticism.

Although Mr. Russell has made valuable contributions to the evolution of thought, I tend to disagree with his views on religion and the nature of life. His ideas on religion, like many other of his contemporaries, are utilitarian. He does not reject religion but proposes that there is class-based adherence to it. He believes the majority, with lower rationality or intellect, pursues a religion for utilitarian objectives of reward and punishment while a small minority with higher knowledge uses it to understand the cosmic scheme of things. His ideas on religion are primitive as he believes that religion has failed to contain the wild instincts of men in achieving moderation and tolerance. Secondly, he attributes the existence of dogma as the failure of a society or to have differences about it to be the fault of religion. To demonstrate this, here are some excerpts from his interview with Alan Watts:

- About the question of morality. The relation of body and mind is much more intimate than is commonly supposed and there is no reason to think that a mind persists when the brain decays.
- As for God well there are a many great arguments have been advanced in favor of the existence of God and one and all I thought and still think that they are invalid and that nobody would have accepted such arguments if they had not wanted to believe the conclusion.
- I don't think that it is certain that there is no such thing as God. I think it is exactly at the same level as the Olympic gods or the Norwegian gods. They also may exist. The gods of Olympics or gods of Valhalla I can't prove they don't, but I think Christian God is no more likelihood than they have. I think they are a bare possibility
- I think most of its (religion) effects in history have been harmful. Not all. Religion causes the Egyptian priests to fix the calendar and to note the occurrence of eclipses so well. In time they were able to predict them. I think those were beneficial effects of religion. But I think great majority have been bad and I think they have been bad because it was held important the people should believe something for which there did not exist good evidence and that falsified everybody's thinking, falsified systems of education and setup also. But I think complete moral error, say namely that it is right to believe certain things and wrong to believe

certain others. Apart from the question whether the things in question are true or false.

- Alan Watts: What is it that makes man ever to demand religion? Bertrand Russell: I think mainly fear. Men feels himself rather powerless. There are three things that cause him to fear when what nature can do to him. It can strike him with lightning or swallow him up in an earthquake. One is what other man can do which is they can kill him in a war. And the third, which has a great deal to do with religion is what his own violent passions may lead him to do the things which he knows in a calm moment he would regret having done. For that reason, most people have a great deal of fear in their lives and religion helps them to be not so frightened by those fears. But with the founder of religions have very little to do with what their followers teach. Very little indeed.
- I think that this present-day religion embodied in the Churches in the main discourages honest thinking and gives importance to things that are not very important. Its sense of importance seems to be quite wrong.
- Alan Watts: What about people who feel they must have faith in a religion otherwise they can't face their life at all? Bertrand Russell: I say people who feel they ought to have faith are showing a cowardice which in any other sphere of life would be contemptible but when it is in the religious sphere it is thought admirable. And I can't admire cowardice in whatever sphere it is.

All the above excerpts refer to dogma rather than religion. He contradicts himself, first rejecting the idea of God but then confesses that he cannot prove there is no God. This attitude towards religion might have been because of his belief that human life is bi-elemental, that is, body and mind. In his view, since the soul cannot be explained, through a scientific method, our identities are defined by the consciousness we achieve in life. It may not entirely be true. The consciousness of each person is indeed unique because of their own experiences, history, and level of education. But there exists a layer of consciousness that is common to all humans. An example could be our experience of tasting salt or sugar that evokes similar experiences of sensations among all members of the human species.

Another perspective could be that life is an interaction of three elements, that is body, mind, and soul. The body is the vessel that has evolved to be able to habitat the earth based on its ecological condition, that is the availability of oxygen, water, and nutrition.

The mind, not just the organ brain, is the repository of all knowledge to which a person gains access through education, experience, and intuition. The level of intellectual consciousness of a person will depend on his unique eagerness to uncover hidden knowledge from the deep recesses of the mind. A plethora of unknowns in the universe suggests that, so far, we have not been able to gain a complete understanding of what is in the mind.

The brain is a biological organ, while the mind at a given moment uses the portion of acquired knowledge to produce consciousness. We don't know precisely where the consciousness resides in the brain. We do know which section of it is activated by each sensory organ and emotions. Higher levels of consciousness are realized, through the application of logic, pure reason, or at least that's what we believe. But in reality, irrational emotions are also part of our awareness and contribute towards our history and identity. We deduce this because a person is, at no point in his existence, deprived of consciously feeling irrational emotions like love, loneliness, sadness, and hate. It is common to all humans, regardless of their careers.

A body and the mind are passive and are not capable of acting or thinking for itself without help from an outside agent. It is like a scientist interacting with the microprocessor and the operating system to produce new research or develop new gadgets.

That agent is the third element soul acting on the body and the mind to produce either kinetic motion or consciousness of the reality of existence. This interaction, with the mind, generates not just awareness but also thoughts that are passive unless the agent acts on it. A person that does not act on these thoughts is considered less inquisitive and hence less intuition. Soul's interaction with these thoughtful inquiries involves constantly acquiring data and facts transmitted through senses and processing it by applying the logic of intellect. It results in intuition that enables the soul to uncover the hidden recesses of the mind and gain access to new insight. The cycle repeats itself throughout our lifespan. The aim of life seems to be to achieve the highest level of consciousness by uncovering the complete knowledge of the mind. In religious terms, prophets have attained that level of heightened awareness and unlocked the mystery of life and the universe.

The soul begins its career at temporal birth. Life is the journey of the soul dealing with the carnal desire, nutritional needs of the body, and the demands of inquiry of the conscious mind that provides every person a unique identity. At the time of death, the body is no longer utilized as a vessel and returned to earth. But the history of the person continues to affect life on earth by their past actions whose consequences are still unfolding. For instance, the outcome of the life of Mr. Russell is still unfolding even after his death, over five decades ago. The extent of these consequences will depend on the kind of existence a person leads. A career that has impacted a large number of people will have consequences unfolding for a longer period of history. Genghis Khan departed at the age of 65, but the impact of his conquests is felt even today after nearly eight centuries. All this will impact the accountability of the person in the afterlife.

Since science does not recognize the soul, it has no comments on what happens to it at the time of death. Religion, on the other hand, informs us that the soul continues to the next stage of its career but in a different dimension where the physical conditions could be different than earth, hence no need for a body. The soul carries with it the history of its career on earth and the knowledge it has acquired. The condition of the soul, in the afterlife, will depend on the level of consciousness attained and held accountable for actions by exercising it. Religion also proposes that being aware of the oneness of God is a necessary condition for being fully aware of oneself, and failure to achieve it will have dire consequences. It should not be surprising because the Creator has that right to be recognized as the originator.

The culmination of the above discussion is that since science deals mostly with the physical world that we live in, it is difficult for it to fully grasp and understand the condition of the soul in an unknown environment after it departs from the body. This anxiety about an unknown future is alleviated by religion that provides some guidance. In the absence of it, the soul will be too restless to live a peaceful life on earth. That is the primary utility of religion for human beings.

***

Science, Philosophy, and Religion

The curiosity to know the real world around us inspires us to contemplate information accumulated through the senses. This data has to be verified countless times, by observers, before considered validated. Science deals with the quantity, measurable quality, and interactions of things around us. It plays the role of an accountant to maintain a record of the natural world and extrapolate it to learn the probability of future events. It does not incorporate anything that cannot be quantified or measured through the tools available to it in the laboratory. It does not allow assimilation of emotions, intuition, and thought as valid parameters to interfere with its accounting. To conclude Maryam-Webster dictionary defines science as: *"knowledge or a system of knowledge covering general truths or the operation of general laws especially as obtained and tested through scientific method"*. It defines the scientific method as *"principles and procedures for the systematic pursuit of knowledge involving the recognition and formulation of a problem, the collection of data through observation and experiment, and the formulation and testing of hypothesis"*.

Philosophy works on a different plane than science. Its domain is concerned with the nature of things. It relies on thought and intuition to work on the empirical evidence available to push the boundaries of science further. It uses both human faculties of emotions and rationality working together to make sense of reality around us. A philosopher is an artist of thought through which he/she builds an abstract idea of a rational concept that is not verifiable through the discipline of science at the time. Philosophical speculation has contributed significantly to our understanding of the world and the underlying principles of nature.

The contemporary state of our human consciousness is a result of historical knowledge that is only a few thousand years old, although science estimates that the universe has been in existence for over 13 billion years. It is a small blip on the vast canvass of the cosmos. It creates a dilemma and uncertainty about relying solely on philosophy and science to provide a holistic view of reality. In the Quran, God talks about the trust bestowed on human beings:

Chapter 33 Verse 72: We did indeed offer the Trust to the Heavens and the Earth and the Mountains; but they refused to undertake it, being afraid thereof: but man undertook it;- He was indeed unjust and foolish;-

The trust referred to in the above verse is probably about the creative ability of men that is the culmination of interplay of free will, intellect, and thought. No other creature can create anything except for what is necessary for their habitat and survival. Men, on the other hand, can create music, paintings, and tools like a space station to extend its abilities. The limitation of men's creativity is that he has to rely on the material around him, but he cannot create something from within himself. Even to create a child, it requires intervention from outside. This power of creating from nothing or from itself is to God alone. Verse 72 of chapter 33 refers to men being unjust because it is this limited creative ability that men use to subjugate other people, declare himself a god, and even create false gods utilizing the material that was itself created by God.

Religion, as the bearer of ultimate truth, tries to fill this void resulting from the inadequacy of science and philosophy. It is concerned with God, and His relations with the creations, on the other hand, philosophy, and science explore the reality of physical existence. In the absence of God, there will be no reality on which these two could work. Religion deals with absolute reality revealed through divine sanction in the form of scriptures. It is difficult for a consciousness that is not yet fully developed to understand the absolute truth revealed by religion. Human beings need to engage in science, philosophy, and religion to have a holistic knowledge of existence. Finding a religion that has been revealed by God, and appreciate its true essence is the most difficult to achieve. It was because of this difficulty that God sent a long series of prophets to impart that knowledge. Greek, Latin American, Indian, African, and Chinese mythology are some examples that demonstrate that in matters of faith, these past generations relied on supernatural phenomena to appreciate the idea of God.

From a utilitarian perspective, religion is concerned with God and His relations with the creations and universe. It considered God significant because He created the cosmos, and everything in it, which is explored by philosophy and science. The discoveries they find is the unveiling of the divine will, are also steps towards confirming one true God. The essence of God is present in all creatures individually, in an association that is unique to each. The idea that personal God is not important is problematic as the creation needs it for its sustenance rather than having an indifferent relation as promoted by pantheism. The omnipotence of God is not a hindrance for an individual to have a personal relationship with Him rather a confirmation that there are multiple layers of His involvement with the creation.

The Quran, as well as other monotheistic faith Christianity and Judaism, narrates the story of the first human Prophet Adam (AS). At the command of God, angels prostrated before the divine will that granted the mind, intellect, and the power to use it to a new creation. It was not prostration before the physical being, made from elements of clay, fire, and air but to the potential it contained. Iblis, an angel of high stature, refused to comply with the command because the vessel made from lower materials did not deserve this stature and committed the sin of arrogance. We can say that it was the first instance of reprimanding a materialistic view of existence. This story suggests the physical evolution of the human species from elements present in the world that was later recognized by the theory of evolution.

The question that now comes to mind is, which religion is a true one? It is a difficult question to answer, and I must qualify it clearly that I respect all faiths. God commands in the Quran that matters of faith are His domain alone, and no one is allowed to judge the other person in this regard. Shirk, believing in deities and idols and associating them with one God, is a sin that will be judged by Him alone. After reading about various religions and talking to its adherents, it seems to me that all religions started with one person, a Prophet, preaching a message. The Quran mentions that prophets appeared for all races and people for guidance and revelation of the true religion. Another interesting observation is that almost all religions started with a belief in one all-powerful God. It was the later generations that contaminated the message by adding ideas to it and distorting the truth, severely undermining the validity of it. Hindus would explain that various material depictions of a deity are many characteristics of one. Zoroastrians suggest that the fire burning in their temples is the light granted to their Prophet by God. It is precisely these later distortions that defines the human condition that the idea of an invisible but all-powerful God is too much to bear for humans because we rely on our senses to understand reality.

Another common trait in many religions is an effort to assign divinity to men and endowing them with extraordinary powers. This phenomenon suggests men's ambition to declare himself a god under various pretexts. Pharaoh of Egypt, who was intoxicated by their worldly power, or Zeus in Greek philosophy possessing mythical skills, or Mansur al Hallaj drunken by his spiritual enlightenment are some of the examples to demonstrate it. Whether it is trinity presented by Christianity or Buddha reincarnated for every generation. Or Hindu worship of human shaped idols to represent various powers of a god. These are distortions driven by human egos. Atheist rejection of a Creator is also derived from human arrogance to reject anything that is beyond our rational comprehension. These examples suggest the deep psychic desire of humans to be godlike and commit shirk in one form or the other. We are uncomfortable to behave just as the creation and have a deep desire to dominate others.

The difference between our similarity and individual uniqueness lies not in physiology or potentialities but psychology and actuality. Our collective wisdom is transferred to each new generation that acts on it to realize the next level of actualization. The evolution of men is not apparent in physical form but our intellectual growth. During this process of progression, at various junctures, we have been sidetracked from this path because of our inability to combine the various competing sources of knowledge. To put us back on track, God has sent Prophets and revealed books periodically.

Sadly, the original revelations, of all contemporary religions are lost, except the Quran. The message of Islam has remained firmly anchored to the revelations of God collected in the Quran. It is this feature that distinguishes

Islam from other religions. It is the collective responsibility of all of us to ensure that the Arabic language Quran is preserved not only for Muslims but for the whole of humanity. Translations can provide an understanding of the message. But it is not a replacement for the original revelation as each language has a different structure and diction which does not convey the exact meaning of the words. It will be better if translations are certified by a competent authority as an acceptable representation. Another practice that has to be carefully applied is the selective quotation of individual verses and their use out of context that creates a perception of contradictions. A better approach is to quote two or three verses preceding or succeeding the verse that contains the main idea to have an appreciation of its relevant background and context.

* * *

Religion and Dogma

We must make a concerted effort to deal separately with religion and dogma. Religion is pursued by an individual to have spiritual elevation to realize self-actualization. Dogma, on the other hand, is a collective social pursuit. It should not be held on par with religion. It is a human enterprise and arises from the subjective interpretation of religious teachings by its scholars. In most situations, the dogma is the accommodation of human fears, greed, and anxieties to develop a version of religion that is more compliant with social needs. It makes the practice of religion simpler for multitude. All religions faced this consequence of transitioning to the dogma once the Prophet had departed. Prophet of Islam, Mohammad (PBUH) understood it and expressed frequent anxiety that his message will face the same crisis, and he was proven right. He expressed this anxiety in his last sermon during the hajj pilgrimage, before his passions away, in the following words:

"All those who listen to me shall pass on my words to others and those to others again; and it may be that the last ones understand my words better than those who listen to me directly."

Dogma is the human interpretation of absolute truths presented by religion.

Since it is a human enterprise, there is a high degree of fallibility built into it. A social contract, from a political perspective, is a form of dogma. The issue arises when developers of a doctrine or those that accept it emphasize that it is for all times and cannot be changed. They fear that changing a dogma will make them depart from the faith, although by adopting it, they have already compromised its purity. Religion is built on infallible truths that are unchangeable. But it uses language as a medium that has subjective limitations because it is a human endeavor. Because of these limitations, human interpretations of revelations cannot necessarily be considered the absolute truth and gives rise to dogma. These subjective understandings of the divine message cannot be applied to the whole society using the coercive power of a State.

Dogma introduces certain inertia that becomes a hurdle in reinterpreting the message of religion. Understanding a revelation should not be frozen in the past. It is because humans are discovering new knowledge that was not available to past generations. For instance, in Christian dogma, it was believed in the medieval era that the sun revolves around the earth. Anyone that proposed that earth revolves around the sun was considered an apostate and subjected to persecution. Muslim scholars debated whether test-tube babies should be acceptable or not. In extreme cases, it is evident that a person pursuing a dogma can defy the very religion that he believes in. We should fearlessly question a dogma because true faith is infallible; we must not forget that.

Would I be a Muslim if I was not born to Muslim parents? And Am I biased towards Islam by considering it a truthful religion because I was born to Muslim parents? Why would someone convert to another religion from Islam if it is a rational religion? I have struggled with these questions for a long time to find a convincing answer. Now I can say with some certainty that I would be a Muslim through personal choice rather than because of an accident of birth. But doubts still linger at the back of my mind as I did not embark on a journey of spiritual enlightenment that a convert does. It is for this reason I kiss the hands of all those who convert to Islam as they found it after a deliberate effort and decided to embark on a path that required sacrificing their family history and creating a new beginning.

In the contemporary era, the struggle is to combine the science of matter, that relates to the physical world, with the science of spirit, that is metaphysics. Since the vessel, our body, is a product of the natural world that is a domain of science, there has been extensive focus on it. One the other hand, the need for spiritual development has been the domain of priests that lack intellectual depth. While scientists agree on the theories they discover adding to their voice, the priests continue to disagree on the principles of the salvation of the soul resulting in weakening their voice by infighting.

Sufis suggest that the origin of all religion is the same. They strive to find similarities in various faiths to counter the influence of materialists. It does not solve the problem as the symbolism of accepting an invisible, one and only, and omnipotent God is also of critical importance because these shapes and forms, of idols, represent ideas that deviate from the path of truth. We must understand that the purpose of the matter is to serve the creation, that means it has a utilitarian objective rather than become dominant even if it is symbolic. On the other hand, the object of the soul is subservience to God that has no apparent temporal existence, and hence it falls prey to suspicion and doubts.

* * *

God's Relation to Men

If political science is about organizing a society, then religious science could be a path to understanding the will of God expressed in the reality around us and our place in this scheme. I am calling religion a science because there is a system, a purpose, and a law by which it is governed just like politics is considered part of social sciences. Newton's laws are concerned with motion and gravity that is experienced by the masses. Similarly, religion is the law governing the relation of men with God based on certain principles. For instance, men can't break out from the reality created for him by God regardless of whether he accepts it or not. He has the authority to express the free will to choose his career within the physical reality but does not have the option to go beyond it. An apple falls on the ground but does not bore the hole in it. Just like the laws of nature and science, principles of religion are set up by God and revealed to prophets to convey to human beings. These laws deal with the soul and its relationship with the creator while experiencing an earthy existence. Religion is difficult to fathom as the ultimate reality is still beyond the reach of science and philosophy. As mentioned earlier, we only have a few thousand years of scientific knowledge, but the universe has been in existence for 13 billion years.

This parallax between the limited physical ability of the body, which contains the soul, and limitless flight of thought creates anxiety, fear, and fascination. It is the creative power of our imagination that enables us to fly in the sky or dive deep in the ocean. But these achievements do not add new capabilities to the body. We have to rely on the use of other elements of nature for it. This awareness of the limitations of the body pushes our imagination to create superhuman like Hercules, Spider-Man, etc. that can dominate forces of nature. That void also gives us a sense that there is something bigger out there. God is the need of men to make sense of the vastness of the universe that can only be probed by the flight of thought. Even the fastest spaceship cannot yet traverse the cosmos to observe it. The certainty of death elevates this anxiety.

The inability to understand and control the universe coupled with the uncertainty of life, when it would encounter death, is too much for humanity to handle. He needs the guiding hand of God to go through this life and deal with these anxieties associated with it. It is the blessing of God that He sent apostles and revealed books to inform, enlighten, and educate men. If God had not helped, men would be lost in the wilderness of his soul and would tear each other apart in this insanity. God is the anchor of humanity.

French philosopher Rene Descartes, in his book *Meditations on First Philosophy*, presents the idea that ".. all things which can exist only in consequence of having been created by God, are in their own nature incorruptible, and can never cease to be, unless God himself, by refusing his concurrence to them, reduce them to nothing..". The decay of things is because of the will of God. It means sustenance and decay happens because of a force exerted by an external agency. Consequently, God is active in the affairs of the world rather than indifferent to it.

Human free will is a privilege, not a right. Men have the independence of action; the outcome of these actions and their consequences are not in his control. Men can analyze the intentions of their actions as there is a conscience built into his nature. By analyzing these options, we know the consequences of our actions and hence are responsible for them. Men will be held accountable for their intentions. It is the prerogative of God alone to allow that the desired acts manifest to produce the desired results. The stories of Prophets Musa (Moses) and Issa (Jesus) are an illustration of it. Prophet Issa (AS) brought people and birds to life by the command of God. He acted while God manifested the desired outcome. When Prophet Musa (AS) struck his staff on the sea, it was God who commanded its parting. Why do we doubt that God could impart these miracles? If we can fly a spacecraft to Mars or develop organs in a lab, then we must not forget God is the original creator. Are we more capable than God?

Obedience or submission to God means to be ready to give up the free will and freedom of choice when instructed. When God commanded Iblis, Satan, to prostrate to Adam (AS), as a creation, he did not have the right to choose but to obey the command. By refusing to obey, Iblis overstepped his status as a creation. Similarly, Adam (AS) was required not to taste the forbidden tree, and it was not his station to ask why not or transgress that limit.

The divine wisdom to seek acceptance of the oneness of an invisible God is to test the intellectual ability of men. The essence of God can be known through logic and reason around us, but it is not evident on the surface as well as require overcoming the ego of the self. This challenge helps to distinguish between those who submit to God and those who retaliated and refused it. It is for this reason that religions that create idols having a shape and form are considered shirk (false association) in Islam. The condition of unquestioned subservience is to believe in an invisible yet omnipresent God without fully comprehending it through reason.

God says that everything in the universe moves or exists by His command. By following its pattern of revolution, around the sun, earth follows the laws of physics. These laws are not created on their own but by God and available for scientists to study. The dark energy and matter that has fascinated the scientists, who do not understand its nature, contribute towards this balance between stars and planets. The same is true for all other living and non-living things to obey the command of God.

In the Quran, God informs men to look around and ponder over the creative energy all around us. But in the process of this quest, a person cannot shout in the marketplace "Ana al Haq" as Mansur al-Hallaj did, nor can he create a figurine symbolically depict God. In this sense, intellect could be a friend to guide a person in his quest to find God or an enemy if it takes hold of the inquiry and require manifestation of God in worldly form or reduced to fit his intellectual limits. When Musa wanted to see God, he got a reply that it is beyond his capacity to be able to sustain it. The test of Adam was also for an unknown tree to be beyond his reach. It required submission to the Divine command and be content with trusting it that not touching that tree was goodness. In the story of Adam, the Divine message is that there is a limit to knowing.

In the Quran, God instructs humanity to strive to explore the universe, and if some of it remains beyond our comprehension, then do not be anxious about it but continue striving. There has to be a balance between knowing and not knowing and being content with it.

The life of a person progresses when something important to him is lost or broken. In that state of despair, the person thinks of new ways to alleviate his distress or misery that then leads to the evolution of the human condition through innovation and art. It is not a sadistic view of life, but the price of creativity. Just like a mother has to go through birth pangs to bring a new life to earth.

* * *

Revelation and Inspiration

Revelation and inspiration are special blessings from God but are different in rank and scope. Divine revelations are a direct communication from God, granting a person the stature of prophet with authority, to define the moral and spiritual code. In political jargon, we can say that prophets introduce legislation. It has to be relayed, verbatim, by the Prophet, without any addition or subtraction. Inspiration from God, on the other hand, is to enable a person to achieve contentment and peace within oneself by finding guidance to resolve a complicated situation or a task at hand. Inspiration does not provide an authority to a person to impose his will on others. Inspiration comes in many forms. Archimedes got it while taking a shower and ran out naked, shouting eureka when he solved the problem of floating bodies. Einstein resolved his theory of relativity while standing on a bridge, watching a train approaching it. Another scientist claimed he solved the chemical equation of a compound in a dream about six monkeys hanging in a particular shape. It is a mysterious world with as many stories as humans themselves.

Before Prophets receive a revelation, they have to go through years of meditations. Prophet Musa (AS) worked as a shepherd for seven years, that is a form of meditation. A shepherd generally loiters around contemplating while the sheep graze the grass. Prophet Mohammad (PBUH) went to a cave for fifteen years to seek the truth. Imagine a person sitting in a cave in complete darkness while there could be lizards or other insects crawling around. It requires a mental focus to meditate in that kind of environment. Prophet Issa (AS) whereabouts were unknown from age 12 to 29, called lost years, of which there is no written record. Some claim, without substantial proof, that he passed through Indian Kashmir during those years. Prophet Ibrahim (AS) traveled through vast distances in deserts to meditate. Each had their way, but they all went through a process of self-cleansing and meditation. The same process of going through meditation is required if any man seeks inspiration to solve a problem, whether it is to understand a scientific puzzle, political dilemma, or personal quest.

Human beings have intellectual limitations in determining a future outcome and controlling all the factors in the present moment that produces an event. For instance, a doctor can't know whether a patient inflicted with cancer will be cured by medicine for sure. He can only predict based on a probability derived from the experience of past patients. These uncertainties of life create anxieties that could be made bearable through prayer. Prayer is not sought by God, but by the humans themselves. It reminds us of our fallibility and limitations. It removes the false sense of superiority and introduces humility that helps us to act justly towards others that are weak in body and social status.

Predestination is beyond human comprehension because a person can't understand the infinite number of possibilities. God, on the other hand, with His divine knowledge, and Wisdom is aware of all possible eventualities and hence the future outcome of events. God can inspire an individual about the future and take action to prevent it. Quran narrates the story of Prophet Musa (AS) and a wise man in the following verses:

Chapter 80 Verses 65 – 82: So they found one of Our servants, on whom We had bestowed Mercy from Ourselves and whom We had taught knowledge from Our own Presence.

Moses said to him: "May I follow thee, on the footing that thou teach me something of the (Higher) Truth which thou hast been taught?"

(The other) said: "Verily thou wilt not be able to have patience with me!"

"And how canst thou have patience about things about which thy understanding is not complete?"

Moses said: "Thou wilt find me, if Allah so will, (truly) patient: nor shall I disobey thee in aught."

The other said: "If then thou wouldst follow me, ask me no questions about anything until I myself speak to thee concerning it."

So they both proceeded: until, when they were in the boat, he scuttled it. Said Moses: "Hast thou scuttled it in order to drown those in it? Truly a strange thing hast thou done!"

He answered: "Did I not tell thee that thou canst have no patience with me?"

Moses said: "Rebuke me not for forgetting, nor grieve me by raising difficulties in my case."

Then they proceeded: until, when they met a young man, he slew him. Moses said: "Hast thou slain an innocent person who had slain none? Truly a foul (unheard of) thing hast thou done!"

He answered: "Did I not tell thee that thou canst have no patience with me?"

(Moses) said: "If ever I ask thee about anything after this, keep me not in thy company: then wouldst thou have received (full) excuse from my side."

Then they proceeded: until, when they came to the inhabitants of a town, they asked them for food, but they refused them hospitality. They found there a wall on the point of falling down, but he set it up straight. (Moses) said: "If thou hadst wished, surely thou couldst have exacted some recompense for it!"

He answered: "This is the parting between me and thee: now will I tell thee the interpretation of (those things) over which thou wast unable to hold patience.

"As for the boat, it belonged to certain men in dire want: they plied on the water: I but wished to render it unserviceable, for there was after them a certain king who seized on every boat by force.

"As for the youth, his parents were people of Faith, and we feared that he would grieve them by obstinate rebellion and ingratitude (to Allah and man).

"So we desired that their Lord would give them in exchange (a son) better in purity (of conduct) and closer in affection.

"As for the wall, it belonged to two youths, orphans, in the Town; there was, beneath it, a buried treasure, to which they were entitled: their father had been a righteous man: So thy Lord desired that they should attain their age of full strength and get out their treasure - a mercy (and favour) from thy Lord. I did it not of my own accord. Such is the interpretation of (those things) over which thou wast unable to hold patience."

In that story, the wise man is authorized by God to take actions to affect the future outcome as a blessing of God for those people. It is an example to show the utility of prayers when an intervention from God is sought, which could ally a misery or pain. In a way, it becomes part of faith to make God the final arbiter of events without holding any remorse for the adversity that happens in our lives.

The story raises some other questions as well. Why did God choose an agent to exercise His will rather than use His divine powers? It is questions like these that have to be analyzed by each generation as our knowledge improves with scientific discoveries. One explanation could be that the presence of a human agent impacts the whole society rather than just the people directly involved. The child that was murdered by the wise one could have died by natural causes that would not have impacted the whole society. Murder, on the other hand, places demand on the community to investigate causes and introduce change to improve their relations.

God, as the supreme authority, has the final say in deciding the course of future events. It is by His permission alone that the future can become a reality. The grant of prayer to human beings is to petition for a favorable response. It is the divine right of God to accept or reject a prayer. Submission to God means to be comfortable that not every prayer will be accepted. Prayer can change the course of future events affecting all of humanity. Imagine over seven billion people, most of them having faith, engaged in prayers result in a large number of probabilities for the future course. That makes it beyond human comprehension or science to predict. The Quran advised in:

Chapter 11, Verse 123: *To Allah do belong the unseen (secrets) of theheavens and the earth, and to Him goeth back every affair (for decision): then worship Him, and put thy trust in Him: and thy Lord is not unmindful of aught that ye do.*

We must not forget that prayer can never be a plan A but rather a plan B to deal with an adverse situation. God has repeatedly instructed that He does not help those who do not help themselves. Chapter 13 Verse 11: *"..Allah does not change a people's lot unless they change what is in their hearts..".*

All evil committed by humans is blamed on Satan, as an outside agency, inspiring us to execute it. In a way, it is human justification to declare himself innocent, and his fallibility is because of the suggestions of Satan. We forget the Quranic story that when the first human, Adam (AS) was introduced, to the Angels, they observed that he would engage in bloodshed and violence.

Chapter 2 Verse 30: Behold, thy Lord said to the angels: "I will create a vicegerent on earth." They said: "Wilt Thou place therein one who will make mischief therein and shed blood?- whilst we do celebrate Thy praises and glorify Thy holy (name)?" He said: "I know what ye know not."

This judgment of angels preceded Satan's refusal to bow down to Adam. It suggests that there is something in the human condition that makes us capable of committing sins and evil, even if there is no Satan. This attitude is the interplay of our physical limitations, desire for spiritual contentment, and intellectual curiosity to take command and control of everything within sight. Nutritional science has advanced to calculate the caloric value of various foods items even though we still consume more than our bodies need physiologically. In this craving for more food, we create food shortages and ignore the hunger of our fellow human beings.

We know that the utility of clothes is to protect our bodies from natural elements. We ignore that basic need and engage in a competition of wearing fashionable clothes that cost so much that a whole town can get nutrition for a month. If we attribute these sins to Satan, rather than to blame our ego to feel superior from others and are driven by greed to have more possessions, then we are fooling ourselves. Satan is not concerned about our food consumption or the quality of our clothes. He is more interested in making sure we commit social sins that damage our relations with other fellow humans. These sins are not physiological but social when we assign partners to God, alleviate someone else to claim to be God or demigod, and commit crimes against humanity.

Universe and Science

Big Bang or Big Expansion

I graduated as an engineer and also completed some science courses to satisfy my curiosity. I cannot claim to be a scientist or an expert in astrophysics. The perspective presented here is the unqualified opinion of a curious person. Since my concern is to understand the relations between God, science, and human nature, it is not possible to ignore these scientific questions about origin of universe.

One of the questions that puzzled scientists is how all this started. The most popular proposal is the Big Bang theory proposed by theoretical physicists. It suggests that the cosmos, and everything in between, came to be when a highly dense matter exploded and set in motion events that eventually produced the universe. There are many unresolved inconsistencies in this theory.

The first unresolved issue is, why did the dense matter explode? Was it an internal dynamic or an external force that made it explode? If it was stable before the Big Bang, then why did it become unstable to explode? A dense matter that bursts by itself, without interference from an outside force, to set the universe in motion will be a closed system. Secondly, science confirms that planetary bodies are moving apart with the speed of light at the macro level, and electrons are revolving around the nucleus at the micro-level. It is only possible when some force is interacting with the matter. What is the source of that force? Recent research on dark matter and dark energy suggests that these unknown phenomena are pushing the universe apart without disturbing the precarious balance required between stars and planets.

Now scientists are proposing another hypothesis of multi-universes.

Everything in the universe is in motion, whether it is galaxies, that are a billion light-years apart, or microscopic electrons. There is nothing static. Here motion does not refer to conversing a distance but a rather continuous change of state that could be a location in space as well as physical characteristics. Time is the accounting measure of this uninterrupted motion experienced by the universe. It creates this dilemma that a dense matter that was not changing its state or static in terms of time explodes for no apparent reason and gives rise to motion and time.

In the context of the Big Bang theory, since everything was static or without change, time did not exist as well. The whole universe started at the bang at the same moment. There should be unity of time in the cosmos, that is synchronization of state of being. That is not the case when we look at the universe through the lens of the theory of relativity. Light from a star that is light-years away reaches us when it has already moved into the future. That should not be the case if the whole universe started at the same time when the bang happened. In other words, time should be independent of space and speed of light.

We know now that the universe is still expanding, which means that the force of gravity should get weaker as planets and stars move away from each other. Since the balance of the universe is not disturbed, despite moving away, that is only possible when a new matter is added. Or an external force provides the extra gravity needed to maintain the balance. If the bang started with dense material, it cannot be unlimited. How is the balance in gravity then maintained despite the expansion of the universe? Some scientists try to answer this question by suggesting that gravity has origin in another universe that is denser than ours. But this external universe should have a changing density as well to provide increasingly higher gravity to our cosmos as it expands.

Another hypothesis is that dark matter converts into the matter to maintain gravity.

As theoretical physicists consider the Big Bang theory to be verified and accepted, they come up with explanations to deal with the above paradoxes.

For instance, the idea of multiple universes or conversion of dark energy into matter.

Now consider what if we refuse the Big Bang theory altogether. If there was no Big Bang, then how did the universe come to be? That is the question we should try to answer through an alternate hypothesis.

We already know that black holes exist in the universe. We do not fully understand the reality of black holes, but we do have evidence of their existence. Now imagine there was no Big Bang of a dense matter but rather a Big Expansion through phenomena like a black hole. It was an expansion like the one when helium is pumped into a balloon. This balloon-like expansion that started at the origination of the universe is adding more matter as inflation continues. It is not an altogether new idea, as some scientists are already thinking about these terms.

This hypothesis of Big Expansion addresses all the four paradoxes mentioned above. In this case, there is no need for a dense matter to explode, and hence there is no need for an explanation where it came from. There is no need for unity of time as each section of the cosmos came to existence at a different moment. As matter passed through the hole, to arrive in the realm of this universe, various sections of the universe came to be. In other words, t0 for each part of the cosmos is different that conforms to the current readings of radiation recorded. Time is relative to each section of the universe. It depends on the moment of its existence, and the duration of time since then. For instance, a section of cosmos that came to the state of being before the Milky Way galaxy has more time-lapsed since its inception, and so is in a different state of change and time. For illustration purposes, consider the example of a father and son. They may exist together at a particular moment in time but are at different stages in their physical selves. Aging or decay is a phenomenon common to everything that exists in the universe.

The laws of physics suggest that matter cannot be created or destroyed but can only change form. As explained in the previous para, since the universe is expanding, new matter is continuously added, through this ongoing process of Big Expansion. As this additional matter is introduced, to this realm, it conforms with the laws and principles prevalent in it. The density and hence force of gravity near the opening of the expansion is high and reduces as it expands. It is this high density at the mouth of this balloon type expansion that explains the source of gravitational force needed to maintain the balance as the universe expands that scientist's reference.

Einstein's theory of relativity breaks down at the moment just before the Big Bang because at that instance, the speed of light was zero that makes both matter and energy 0 if the equation e=m(c square) is to be valid. That means nothing existed, and if nothing existed, then it cannot explode. But the theory remains valid if there was a Big Expansion. Through this Big Expansion, the universe started in motion rather than changing its state from stationary to being in motion that was proposed by Big Bang theory. Consequently, it was never in a static state. It has always been in a continuous state of change at every level of existence.

The dark matter and dark energy that is prevalent throughout the universe originates because there is an active force that is being applied, through the black hole from which this universe came to be. It is still producing more matter and continuing the expansion.

The event of the Big Expansion could have started at approximately 13 billion years as estimated by Scientists based on the radiation recorded by them.

* * *

Definition of Time

Merriam-Webster's dictionary defines time in many ways. Some of it is as follows:

1. The measured or measurable period during which an action, process or condition exists or continues.
2. A non-spatial continuum that is measured in terms of events which succeed one another from past through present to future.
3. An appointed, fixed, or customary moment or hour for something to happen, begin, or end.

Defining time has puzzled philosophers and scientists alike. As illustrated above, the definition of time is a lapse of duration between events. The problem with this definition is that it creates different times throughout the universe, depending on the subjective location of an observer or estimator of it. A person holding a stopwatch on earth, moon, mars, or another galaxy will report different times. Similarly, a star two lunar years away is considered to be moved to the future when the light emitted by it reaches earth. It means that our understanding of time distance and speed play a role as well. Everything in the Universe emanates from a single event which we call a Big Expansion as the Quran suggests it in Chapter 2 Verse 117 "…He saith to it: 'Be'. And it is". If it is true, then time throughout the universe should be synchronized or unified independent of the location of an object or observer. How do we solve this paradox?

The creation of the universe is an event that has not finished yet and is still unfolding. In this ongoing event, time is the unique state of the cosmos at a particular moment. This state is the cumulative condition of everything that includes celestial bodies, a virus, or a particle of dust resting on a stone. Everything in the universe affects each other, and they form a unified whole. An ant carrying a piece of grain is as relevant, to us, as a dust particle removed from the surface of a stone by the wind. Each state is unique in its composition from the one preceding or succeeding it.

Time, as an accountant of change, cannot exist in an absolute vacuum regardless of its size because there is no change of state from one moment to the other. The vacuum does not exist in the universe as there is dark matter and energy present in all points of space. Time, to be independent of an observer, is neither a rate of change of state from one moment to another nor is it the measure of duration between two events. It is a unique state of the universe at a particular moment.

Time is like a movie that is a continuous presentation of still impressions on a canvas. Each still is unique. When they are displayed, in continuity, we experience the motion of the characters or things. If we present stills of the movie out of sync, meaning they are shown in random rather than in a sequence, then we cannot perceive a comprehensible motion. Just like a movie, the moments follow each other in succession for it to appear continuous to our sensory perception. The duration is a set of moments in a continuum. For instance, while watching a movie, we can watch a particular two-minute duration segment that is different from other parts.

How long a moment is depending on the speed of change. If no change occurs, time will stand still and not progress to the next moment. Our worldly watches record duration by calculating the oscillation of an atom for a certain number of times. When we look at the universe, a better watch could be one that records the change in the state or condition of an entity. For instance, there are two entities A and B. Now imagine, an entity A changes to A+1 while entity B remains the same with no change. For an observer that watches A and B, it would appear that A has duration while B does not or absence of lapse of time in its state for the observer. Imagine you are watching a video and a photo. In a video, you can experience the lapse of time, by slowing or fast-forwarding the video, but in a photo, time is still and not moving. If the life around us was a still picture, time would stop.

This change in state is not just movement through distance but also changes in the condition of an entity. For instance, from the human perspective, aging is the change of state and gives us a perception of time if everything else in the universe remains the same. Synchronization of the clock does not mean every point in the cosmos has the same time clock. It is rather the state of change they are experiencing relative to their existence with other things in the cosmos. In other words, it means that synchronization in the universe is related to the state of change of various entities existing at that moment. Each moment of time is defined by this unique record of the state of the universe at that very instance. As soon as a change of state happens, we are in the next moment. Variation in the state involves both autonomous changes, like the earth revolving around the Sun, and voluntary change, such as when a person starts a car or moves his hand. A moment is a sum of all the states resulting from the voluntary and autonomous change.

Time is the record of motion, space, or distance as these are states of entities. It is the only way there could be a unity of time, at different points in the universe. From this concept of time, it is not concerned about the speed of a ray of light. It means that its position in space and state is relevant rather than the distance it has traveled from one moment to the other. Imagine a ray of light emitted from a far-off star, say two lunar years away. When it is observed, on earth, it conveys information about the star at that particular moment in time. So, there is unity or, in other words, synchronization of time in the universe as it is independent of motion, space, and distance. The Big expansion hypothesis we presented in the preceding pages also suggests this as each part of the universe is at a different state of being depending on its moment of emergence in the current realm. A clock to record time is dependent on the observer. As each observer, except God, has a limited domain, the watch is also limited in its measurement of time. God is the ultimate timekeeper, as explained above, while our watches, help us, record time to synchronize our lives with others and to measure our performance.

From a utilitarian perspective, time provides a source of audit and accounting for each living and nonliving thing in the universe. A person knows his or her particular state at a given moment in time, but they cannot comprehend the exact state of all other things that are within their domain of observation. Only God has the perfect measure of each moment as He is the only one aware of the exact state of all things in the universe.

Humans can exercise their free will that means they have the power to change things around them to define the next moment. The scope and extent of this power are not more than an electron revolving around a nucleus in an atom. We impact things that are minuscule as compared to the number of probabilities that exist. We must remember this when we inflate our egos for our achievements. In spiritual terms, the state of the next moment is only in control of God as only He has the power to allow or stop the universe to change from one state to another from one moment to the next.

In computers, there is a concept of the system clock. All components of the computer function as they are in sync because of it, and if this clock malfunctions whole system comes crashing down. It was this system clock that created the millennium risk for programmers when the world entered the 21st century, and there was a fear that all systems may not sync harmoniously. By using this example of computers, the larger question is, where is the system clock for the universe? How does it sync with everything in the cosmos? Is this system clock dependent on the speed of light? These are questions that might be able to shed some light on the creation of the universe and whether it was a Big Expansion commanded by God.

* * *

Pragmatism of Science and Evolution

Oxford dictionary defines science as: "the intellectual and practical activity encompassing the systematic study of the structure and behavior of the physical and natural world through observation and experiment."

Scientists start their research by exploring the question of why things are the way they are. But in the end, settle with the findings of how to explain or record a phenomenon. The scientific information we have about how things are is not answering an 'a priori' but rather an observation of attributes exhibited without knowing the starting source of it. The foundation of science is hinged on probability, uniformity, and statistics. In this approach, it is a foregone conclusion that if something has happened repeatedly in the past, then the chance of it happening again in the future is high. But it is mere speculation with a high degree of confidence that it will happen. For instance, we know the sun rises every day. We can speculate with a high degree of assurance, deducted from the past observation, that it will rise again tomorrow.

But this probability cannot be 100% because we do not know with absolute certainty how this past behavior was acquired by the sun in the first place. Because of this uncertainty, we cannot be sure to say that we fully understand the principles based on which this behavior was acquired that introduces a slight deduction in our probability even though it may be an insignificant fraction. This dilemma arises when we have to examine space before all this starts. In that space, there was no existence of gravity because there was no matter the way we know it. After the Big Bang or Big Expansion, as we propose, the elements emerged with specific physical characteristics for it to have the effect of gravity.

Scientists know that the laws formulated by them are as good as the empirical evidence known to them at that particular time unless some more facts discovered, after further research, that negates it. For instance, people believed the world is flat until later facts revealed it is round. Others concluded; it is stationary with the sun revolves around it until we found that is not the case. History is replete with examples of scientific theories that were revoked after new evidence emerged. Recent discoveries are shedding light on dark matter and energy, and yet their exact nature is unknown. Despite this uncertainty about absolute reality, scientists adopt an approach that can, at best be, termed as pragmatism.

The expression of the natural world is categorized by scientists using different mediums like Mathematics, Physics, Chemistry, or Biology. But in effect, all these approaches have to represent one true nature of things from different angles. For instance, the mathematical model of an iron atom should be the same as its physical characteristics or its chemical representations. A contradiction in any one of these expressions would mean that they are not representing the true nature of an iron atom.

The cornerstone of the foundation of the theory of evolution is that over time the genes will mutate to form new species. Why did this mutation happen? The most convenient answer is that it is a chance occurrence in response to external changes in the environment to survive. In other words, the development of all the sophisticated species is mostly by chance. The next question that comes to mind is that some of these species might be unnecessary or redundant as a chance occurrence can be a mistake as well. Can we say that the extinction of dinosaurs was because nature realized it was a wrong creation disturbing the balance? It would suggest that there was no ecological balance at that time. It then leads to the question that was there ever an ecological equilibrium as old species become extinct and new species emerge without a break. Is climate change of today just another of those events of imbalance in the history of the world?

It raises the question of whether nature itself is capable of making an intelligent decision or is there an external force that works on it. Pantheistic belief in mother nature being self-sufficient is filled with flaws because it did not give rise to the Big Bang, or Big Expansion. It exists as a consequence of it. Nature is an agent, not a principal in the scheme of things around us. Can an agent then have the capability to make intelligent decisions to create itself? It seems highly unlikely and requires a principal agent to act. The other way to look at it is that the creation is part of a plan and scheme that is well thought out and not just a chance occurrence. It also means that the natural world has to conform to the principles, laws, and rules designed for it to exist. The creator never ceased to create. The role of science is to explore and understand the natural world for the benefit of humanity.

Does nature have emotions or consciousness? From the evolutionary point of view, it has to have it because it cannot grant something to the creatures living in it if it does not have it within itself. All living creatures act in a predictable behavioral pattern except for humans that have the capacity and capability to adopt a career that defies their physical limitations. For instance, an animal that does not know how to swim submerged cannot do it, but humans can by using the elements in nature to their advantage. This advanced knowledge about the environment, and the ability to manipulate it, is only the domain of humanity while all other animals are limited in this capacity. This superiority of humans is even though many animals, for instance, crocodiles, have existed on the earth for far longer than humans. Why is this difference in the intellectual and creative capabilities of creatures? What happened, and at what point there was a sudden spike in the evolution of human consciousness. Why was no such spike, in potential, experienced by any other species? These are puzzling questions and another challenge to evolutionary scientists who refuse to accept the possibility of divine intervention to further human knowledge through intuition and revelation.

Another angle from which to look at evolution is the ability to produce art. Artists first visualized abstract ideas that were later converted to working tools by scientists. Most of us have seen the Leonardo Da Vinci drawings of a machine similar to a helicopter. Why is it that other animals are devoid of producing varied forms of art? Although most animals do have some capability of producing art like birds that sing or dolphins that perform acrobatics or peacocks that dance. But this is no match to the depth and diversity of human artistry.

Artistic expression is not possible without emotions that, in turn, are not possible without consciousness of self and others. A biologist may describe human emotions as an outcome of chemical changes in the body, but what triggers those changes and why is still unknown to us. The science of human psychology that studies our emotional nature is still in its infancy. Experiencing God is an emotional event, and probably one more reason for science's inability to fully appreciate it.

Yet another challenge thrown at evolutionary scientists is the ability of humans to have a diversity of culture as compared to all other species. Animals and plants also experience cultures but not as varied and detailed as humans. Animals have a particular diet that satisfies their hunger, but humans require not only food but elaborate cuisine that has a unique quality to it. Similar is the adoption of dress to cover oneself because of the cultural consciousness to have shame in being naked. Why is it that animals don't feel shame in not covering themselves? It is these differences that nature is unable to define in the absence of a Creator. Religious people would say that existence and evolution is the result of intelligent design and the result of an invisible hand of a creator.

The discipline of science is built based on sensory evidence that is considered as undeniable facts to arrive at conclusions. Almost all instruments to gather data are built using sensory principles. God cannot be observed using the sensory organs except when He revealed his essence to some prophets. He is a phenomenon that exists beyond the realm of human comprehension of reality that makes Him inaccessible to the experimentation of science. The immense and incomprehensible nature of God makes Him an unacceptable agent to scientists, although most of them are neither atheist nor agnostic. God wants all of us to experience His existence that is only possible through keeping our curiosity alive. He wants us to try to find answers to questions about why things are the way they are rather than being satisfied with the narrow realization of how things happen in nature.

Science is work in progress, but God has been present in human consciousness since the recording of history. It is impossible to fully experience humanity without engaging in an emotional struggle about finding God whether a person believes in Him or not.

* * *

Reformation of Science

One of the fascinating aspects of our existence is how we perceive things and the foundation of our consciousness. There are two layers of perception which we can call objective and subjective. Objective perception is common to all humans, for example, watching white color or the sky. Subjective perception is unique as an emotional association with an object that varies with the unique experiences of each individual. Each person watching a table will agree about what it is, but the two people may not have the same emotional association with it. A master or a servant will have a differing emotional association with a table. Another association could be the carpenter who made the table, and a buyer will have a different sentimental association that affects our consciousness of perceiving it.

Another puzzle in this equation is that each species has their unique perception and awareness that is different from all others. Allow me to expand on this thought. We know that a fly sees our hand moving in slow motion. Scientists attribute this to the difference in heartbeats that is 370 beats per minute for a fly, which is about five times faster than a human being. The eye structure of the fly is also much different from humans. It enables a fly to process the light striking her eyes faster than us as well as gathering data using complex eye structure.

The limitation of science is that its edifice rests on our sense perception. Philosophers have been grappling with this limitation for ages. What it means is that the bulk of the scientific discoveries and theories are an outcome of observations made in a lab using five senses of smell, sight, sound, touch, and taste. Even the lab instruments are designed based on these sense perceptions. An electron microscope helps us see at a micro level that is not visible to the naked eye. In a way, it extends the vision of the eye just like a telescope does to see objects at a far-off distance.

This reliance on sense perceptions has served humanity well and resulted in our ability to master the matter to improve our lifestyles. But since observations are deductions using a trial-and-error method, we cannot say for sure that we know the exact nature of things. Side effects of these manufactured products like pollution are indicative of that point. If we knew the absolute nature of diesel fuel, we would be able to design an engine that does not discharge a residue that pollutes the air. It means there is something about the nature of diesel as a fuel that is still not understood correctly. Another example is our medicines can cure one ailment while damaging something else in the body as a side effect.

Even the development of mathematics, as a scientific language, is an attempt to give sense perception to abstract ideas. It is the medium that helped to convert philosophical metaphysical ideas into theoretical physics. Mathematical models of theoretical physics enabled us to accept them as valid and verified. Electrons at the subatomic level or gravity at the extraterrestrial scale, could not have been possible to perceive in the absence of mathematics. Mathematics is classified as synthetic knowledge that is independent of analytical exercise and hence an 'a priori'. The mathematical a priori, that two plus two is four, is about a consciousness that there is an idea four that is both dependent on its components and independent of it. That would mean that learning mathematics is bringing this hidden knowledge from the subconscious to the conscious to be able to make use of it. Now consider that a priori of the mathematical idea four is not in the consciousness of an animal, or even if it does, there seems to be no utility for it. An animal is indifferent to the idea of four, but a human is not. The existence of an 'a priori' alone is not enough but has to interact with the cognitive ability to understand the knowledge, and then there has to be an agency that can act on it.

Mathematical models of the natural world are approximations. We cannot say that they depict the absolute or entire reality of these phenomena. Imagine a mathematical formula that explains the natural world like two plus two is equal to four without any doubt about it. That would be the ultimate goal of science to achieve but is yet beyond our reach. Mathematical models do not provide any clues as to why an electron needed to appear in the first place. Is it possible to create some other particle that can replace electrons or a combination of particles that could create the atomic balance needed for a stable atom but are different than electrons? Science, in most cases, assumes that things or events happened by chance rather than a plan. It is quite amazing to assume that a complex system arising from these chance happenstances could operate so harmoniously and defies the logic. Our view of the matter is from the utilitarian perspective rather than the larger scheme of things. Humanity is concerned with benefiting itself rather than creating selflessly.

The question then is, what is the best way to approach science? It is not an easy question to answer. But one way to approach it could be to understand the process of creation by which diesel, for example, came to be and why it came to be. I mean, why was it necessary for nature to combine the elements of carbon and hydrogen in a particular format and structure to produce diesel.

The branch of knowledge that could contribute to redefining the scientific foundation is the advancement in understanding the ecological system. This branch of science got a boost from our desire to find information about the damage caused by industrial waste. This information can be applied to understand the purpose of the creation of elements and species towards maintaining the natural balance. We can develop computer models that can study the impact of removing, for example, copper from earth. It will help us understand the purpose of having copper in the environment. I will try to elaborate on this point in the remainder of this chapter.

Imagine a light reflected by an object that creates a sensation of white color in our consciousness. The scientific explanation will be that when the ray of light struck the surface of the object, all other frequencies were absorbed by it, and only the wavelength associated with white color light was allowed to reflect that reached our eyes. It means that the whiteness of the object is the feature of the light, not the object itself. In other words, the object has in it all other colors and rejected the white color that, in a way, is deception rather than the reality of it. Now the other thing to consider is that every time that particular frequency of light enters our eyes, we become conscious of the color white.

The consciousness of experiencing white has to be an 'a priori' as the optical nerve does not do anything but convey information about the type of frequency of light. Suppose a creature A has an eye that captures sensory data from a wavelength of light to produce signals to the brain that perceives it as a white color in the consciousness. Now imagine creature B that has a different eye structure that captures sensory data from the same frequency of light to produce signals to the brain that perceives it as a blue color in the consciousness. The point is that the sensation of color arising from the sense data gathered from the same light source will depend on the structure of sense organ that records it and the corresponding brain structure that will give rise to a particular consciousness related to the creature. An apple that appears red to us may appear blue for another species. The material on which the light strikes make changes in the wave of light. We cannot say that the matter has the color white, all we can say is that a certain type of material always makes a particular change in the wave of light. When this altered light strikes our sensory data collection organ, it sends the signal to the brain that perceives white color as it corresponds to that type of wave of light. A sensory data collection organ of a different specification, for example, a bee, or an owl, could send a signal to the brain that perceives it as maybe a different shade of white. So, the color is not in the matter but outside it.

Let us look at it from another angle. Imagine a person that does not have sight or hearing at birth. We choose these two senses because it is rare that someone is impaired to have no sense of smell, taste, or touch. How does a person that does not have access to sight acquire knowledge about objects or colors? When we tell a blind person, there is a table in a room, what image appears in their consciousness? Is that image similar to the table or different in structure? When we tell a blind person about the color red, what is their perception of it? If these perceptions were not close to real-life objects, then it would be quite difficult for a blind person to have a normative function and be intellectually capable. There is sufficient evidence to suggest a blind person has the same intellectual capability as anyone else. It is only possible when the consciousness of objects is an a priori.

Let us try to look at the scientific discoveries assuming preconception is an a priori in human condition because, in the absence of it, the possibility of teaching a language and developing other faculties in a child will not be there. In that case, we would have to evolve a unique educational syllabus for each child. These diversely educated children will not be socially capable of forming a functioning community. Let me try to elaborate on this point using computers as an example. When you buy Microsoft or Apple computers, each comes with a unique operating system. The operating system (OS) is needed by all computer systems, so that we can call their level of consciousness while the files created by a user are the unique history of each of these devices. A computer file created on a Microsoft OS cannot be used on an Apple computer since the two operating systems are different. The consciousness of Microsoft computers will not be able to understand the files created using the consciousness of an Apple OS computer. We would have to build a software interface to help with that. The point is that it will not be possible to teach the subjects of physics, chemistry, mathematics, and biology to all the children until and unless they all had the same operating system.

Now let us refer again to the story of the fly. The image of an object seen by a fly may be different than the image seen by humans although all flies may see it the same way. That means the reality of a fly is different from that of a human. The operating system, consciousness, of a fly is a different one from human beings. It means that its understanding of laws and principles is unique to itself. A fly will have to develop a computer that can interact with its intellect and consciousness. If we could interpret the laws of physics regarding a fly or a tiger, then we might be able to find new knowledge that might be different than our own. If we say a human is a Microsoft OS, and a fly is an Apple OS computer then we would need a file converter to achieve this objective.

Understanding and accessing that inbuilt operating system of a human being or any other species can give us access to data that is not generated by the five senses or help us look at data in a much more different manner. We have to develop a genetic code of consciousness, just like we have deciphered the physical attributes of a human being through a genome project. Considering the example of the computer, we still do not know whether the brain is the random-access memory (RAM)/read only memory (ROM) or the central processor. We also don't know exactly where the operating system of a human being is stored.

Advancement in genetics and psychology could provide clues to gain access to a better understanding of humans and their intellect. For instance, finding a scientific explanation for dreams and intuition could unlock some of the mysteries. From the human genome project, we already know that genes carry propensity to certain illnesses of the parents to the next generation. That could also mean that wisdom and acquired data or knowledge can potentially be passed on to the next generation. One interesting research project would be to find the gene of knowledge and learn from it.

I usually tell my friends that there are limits to how high an airplane can go, but we should not put any restrictions on how high our imagination can fly. We need some out of the box thinking to reform scientific thinking and elevate it to a new level.

Human Consciousness and Reality

Awareness of Self

French philosopher Rene Descartes suggested that the sure sign of existence is that a person is conscious of his reality. It should apply to both humans and other living entities, that is animals, insects, and plants. Co-related to this was the concept that there is only one thing we all can be sure of, that is our existence. All other things around us could be a delusion of the senses and should be dealt with a fair dose of skepticism. Imagine you are sitting in a room watching things around you. To the naked eye, objects in the room like chairs, tables, vases, etc. are real and have an existence in physical time and space. While sitting in the same room you watch things on a three-dimensional virtual reality (VR) headset. These same things that are real in the room are not present anymore as they don't exist inside the VR headset but are just an impression of it. It creates a degree of uncertainty for consciousness, whether the things in the room are also an impression than reality.

I mentioned the above concept for a particular reason that will become clear to you as we continue exploring it. When a child is born, he carries the DNA of parents. The body is the product of this genetic code of the parents helping the child acquire similar facial features, the texture of hair, skin color, height, etc. from the parents. The body may carry imperfections as well. Parents also provide emotional content through the history of upbringing. The child may even retain the knowledge acquired by his parents, hidden in the unconsciousness. The soul is a different matter altogether because we do not yet fully understand its nature. At its creation, this new soul is pure and perfect without any faults or defects. It arrives with its unique possibilities for the future. It is like a blank slate.

An infant is a brand-new entity having a mind that is mostly sleeping, a body that is growing, and a soul that is getting ready for a new journey. With each passing day, this new soul starts accruing obligations towards his parents and other people who share care for him. It slowly adopts the culture and religious dogma of his parents. His teachers help develop the faculties for him to experience a career. To learn all these things requires time. The time needed by a person to reach adulthood is one of the longest among all animals, that is 15-18 years.

But when it grows fully to be an adult, the challenges start for this person. He is now accountable for his actions. He has to decide what kind of life he wants to live. He can pursue the faith, the religion of his parents or personal exploration to find the true faith or no faith; a lifestyle of righteousness or fraud; and career to serve humanity or take away from it for personal satisfaction. All these actions become part of the history of this soul. At the end of the journey, the soul returns to where it came from. It carries, to the afterlife, the consequences of actions and to account for it.

The Quran says clearly that each person has to answer for his actions and will not be granted any favors for being born to noble parents. There are many verses about it like the one below:

Chapter 34 Verse 37: And it is not your wealth, nor your children that bring you nearer to Us (i.e. please Allah), but only he who believes (in the Islamic Monotheism), and doesrighteousdeeds (will please Us); as for such, there will be twofold reward for what they did, and they will reside in the high dwellings (Paradise) in peace and security.

In these stories, we have examples of Prophets whose sons or brothers were Prophets as well, for instance, Dawood & Suleiman (AS), Yaqoob & Yousuf (AS), Musa & Haroon (AS) and Ibrahim & his sons Ishaq & Ismail (AS). But at the same time, we have the examples of the son of Noah (AS); father of Ibrahim (AS); and uncles of Prophet Mohammad (SAW) who refused to accept the faith. The message is that lineage does not guarantee anything. Each person has to embark on his quest regardless of who his parents were.

How does this apply in the political arena? It means politicians should not tell us about their lineage. They should inform us who they are and what they can do for the community. They should tell us whether they have been a responsible citizen or not in terms of respecting rules, laws, and paying their due share of taxes. And if they have a bad reputation, among the majority of constituents, it is most likely they are bad whether a court of law has convicted them or not. Because the good or bad standing of a person is a result of countless acts of small injustices and insults, they have meted out to their neighbors and acquaintances. If their constituents cannot trust them, then they cannot be reliable in governing the state as well.

Political evolution has worked in tandem with scientific discoveries. The revolution in communication and processing technologies helped store vast amounts of data to be stored online and made accessible to people. The miniaturization of components and productivity enhancement brought the cost of production down, making it affordable for children of the lower middle class to access knowledge and become empowered. It helped in the democratization of societies and overthrow of autocratic governments. Humanity has not yet achieved the ultimate objective of eradicating poverty, ensured equality, and removed class bias. It is still a work in progress.

* * *

Philosophy of Happiness

In the West, consumerism has taken away the motivation to pay attention to self and forget about the anxieties of life. But these anxieties do not go away as consumption itself creates a hangover. In some underdeveloped countries, these anxieties are more pronounced, resulting from terrorism, social injustice, and no rule of law. These constant reminders of risks have heightened the animal's instincts for survival. In this state, the ability to think of collective good breaks down, and a person is more concerned about their self-interest. It is for this reason that our moral threshold has dissipated. They do not feel ashamed of taking a bribe; cheat on the tax return; steal electricity; steal jobs from the right candidate and seek accolades and titles that can enhance our social status or political power without really deserving it. A consequence of these cravings is a never-ending vicious cycle of turmoil and break down of social values. This ceaseless thirst for self-satisfaction at the cost of others morphs into an abnormal society, and it seems this phenomenon is spreading around the world as war, terrorism, and pandemic lingers on.

It seems the revolution in communication technologies has brought all of us closer to each other regardless of the physical distance. At the same time, the overload of communication has taken time away to reflect on oneself. We are getting more and more distanced from our inner self that is producing anxieties. This psychological condition, in some rare cases, becomes fatal like many incidents of mass shootings, in the USA, by young teenage shooters. The worry, about death and possible sickness, is always at the back of our mind. It does not alleviate even if we keep ourselves lost in enjoyment at any given moment in time. Another anxiety that impinges upon us is the awareness of fading away from existence that is further aggravated by the frivolity of whatever we do in life. It leads to another deep-seated concern to understand the meaning of existence. The question we should explore is whether the definition of happiness has changed over the recorded history of philosophy. I wanted to share what other philosophers have defined happiness.

Greek philosopher, Socrates (died 399 BC) felt that self-confidence, which leads to contentment, is achieved when a person does not hesitate to raise questions about the validity of the opinion of others. He did not suggest that these queries are meant to discredit the majority opinions but rather that humans tend to adopt a herd mentality and follow those, without questioning, that have political or financial influence. This tendency to conformity invades individual liberties and ideas so much so that any difference in opinion is considered fatal to the existence of traditional society. He was convicted, by a citizen's court, for these provocative thoughts by being condemned to death by a jury of 500 for creating social unrest. Those that punished him perished without a trace, but Socrates and his self-confidence live on proving his point.

Another Greek philosopher, Epicurus (341-270 BC), on the other hand, proposed that happiness is attained through the interaction of the company of good friends, freedom, and an ability for self-reflection. He suggested that money loses its validity as a source of happiness once a person attains a level of subsistence. He considered reflection as a relevant tool to deal with the anxieties of life.

Roman stoic philosopher, Lucius Seneca (died 65 AD) was more concerned with a heightened state of emotions, especially anger. He considered rage an outcome of shattered expectations. He suggested that the ability to deal with anger can be improved when a person lowers their expectations and to be always adapted for an unexpected adverse outcome.

Philosopher of French Renaissance, Michel de Montaigne (1533-1592 CE) presented the views that a person has to deal with three kinds of inadequacies most of their life. These are physical, cultural, and intellectual inadequacies. Physical inadequacies like balding, facial hair, the color of skin, etc. develop a personality complex that has a direct influence on the contentment and happiness of a person. Similarly, acting in a manner that is considered culturally abnormal can also result in personal anxieties like blowing nose in public. Intellectual inadequacy is related to the ability of a person to appear intelligent and knowledgeable. Montaigne presented the idea that it is all too humane to have any of these inadequacies. A Wise-man is one who can contain anxieties arising from these concerns.

German philosopher Frederick Nietzsche proposed that failures and challenges of life prepare for a higher objective that is not yet encountered by a person. His own life was a living example of it. He struggled with schizophrenia for most of his adult life and spent the last 10 years in total mental oblivion. A distorted view of his philosophy was used by Nazis to gain popular support.

South Asian philosopher-poet, Allama Muhammad Iqbal, advised us that exploration of self is the path to contentment, enlightenment, and understanding the purpose of life. He proposes that all answers to the questions posed by the outside world can be found inside a person. He feels that the elevation of the self enables the person to connect with the divine that is the real source of enlightenment, empowerment, and contentment. His idea of self-consciousness is like the sense of freedom proposed by Epicurus as one of the three things that make us happy.

In religious terms, prayer is a reflection on oneself and having a conversation with the Creator. Prayer is meditation in which a person can engage in a conscious dialogue with the Creator to understand the meaning of life and the anxieties associated with it. As a blessing, God answers in response to this prayer in the form of intuition and inspiration, it is for personal consumption and not to be imposed on other people as a dogma or taken material benefit from it. This conversation with God liberates the soul from the shackles of anxieties with the realization that they do not define the whole life and creates hope for the future. Prayer is not an escape from the responsibility of living a life or procrastination from trying to solve the issues faced by us. It is an acceptance of the limitations of a human experience that does not have the power to control the events around us. The free will granted to us has boundaries that end within ourselves.

How do we become a normative society? The solution cannot be only with the government or politics or a growing economy. The key is within us. All of us must individually realize that protecting and safeguarding each other enriches our own lives. We comprehend that being part of injustice in any shape or form, in the end, affects our lives and not just the lives of the oppressed. An unjust society prevents happiness of self. Both oppressed and oppressor are like conjoined twins. Happiness is derived from the contentment of the conscience and doing something for the other person.

* * *

Reality and Evolution

Dr. Jeffery Lang, professor of Mathematics at the University of Kansas, narrated his story of conversion to Islam. He referred to the story of Prophet Adam (AS) presented by the Quran in the following verses:

Chapter 2 Verse 35-39: And We said: "Oadam! Dwell you and your wife in the Paradise and eat both of you freely with pleasure and delight, of things therein as wherever you will, but come not near this tree or you both will be of the Zalimun (wrong-doers)." Then did Satan make them slip from the (garden), and get them out of the state (of felicity) in which they had been. We said: "Get ye down, all (ye people), with enmity between yourselves. On earth will be your dwelling-place and your means of livelihood - for a time." Then learnt Adam from his Lord words of inspiration, and his Lord Turned towards him; for He is Oft-Returning, Most Merciful. We said: "Get ye down all from here; and if, as is sure, there comes to you Guidance from me, whosoever follows My guidance, on them shall be no fear, nor shall they grieve. "But those who reject Faith and belie Our Signs, they shall be companions of the Fire; they shall abide therein."

He wondered that when Prophet Adam (AS) transgressed by tasting from the forbidden tree in heaven, the punishment he got was to live on a planet on which there were provisions for him for all his needs. He questioned what kind of punishment it was when provisions for sustainable life were made available. It is an interesting point to ponder over. The real punishment for Prophet Adam (AS) was a deprivation of his high consciousness, that was made hidden under many layers, and a direct consequence of it was impairment of reality. In the absence of this comprehension of reality, humans prefer to deal with faulty notions and lack of understanding of the world around us. So, what is the reality? How can we ascertain it? We discussed it briefly in the previous chapter and will try to tackle this question as much as we can.

Scientifically life emerged from physical matter that means that there is a potential of life in it just like the potential of a tree in a seed. In other words, the difference between living and non-living things is consciousness. From this perspective, physical features should not define a species but the expression of its consciousness. If the consciousness of a dog is the same as a human, can we then call it a dog despite its physical shape may be such? The difference between a person and a dog is the differences not just in physical features but also in consciousness. From a religious perspective, the Quran confirms that a process of evolution started when God said to be. Chapter 36 Verse 82: "Verily, when He intends, a thing, His command is to 'be', and it is!". It was a divine decision that the consciousness of each species acquired a particularly unique characteristic. Each creature is in its perfect state, and there is no fault in it. It means that dogs are in their impeccable form and cannot be improved further. The same is true for a lion or a giraffe.

When we look at an iron bar, we perceive its reality through our five senses. Our eyes provide us with information about its physical dimensions and other features. Through touch, we know that it is a hard metal. We know it is not emitting any sound as we do not hear anything when we take our ear near it. It has no smell as we do not sense any. And it does not have any particular taste unique to it. But is this the truthful reality of the iron bar? When we put the same iron bar under a microscope, we find out that it is not that solid but rather hollow as there are wide spaces between the atoms. So, we adjust our understanding of the reality of it and say that being solid is an appearance rather than a final reality. This inability of senses to convey absolute reality raises a lot of questions. Do they facilitate knowing the truth, or become a hindrance in the quest for it? Are they a challenge to be overcome so that we can differentiate between the levels of consciousness of people? Or a starting point to initiate a journey of awareness?

From this simple example, we can say that the consciousness of reality has multiple layers, and we cannot rely on our senses alone to understand it. It also suggests that to find the truth, we have to work harder rather than take it for granted. The absolute reality should be objective and independent of the observer. Now suppose a person attains knowledge of absolute reality, will he/she be able to communicate it to others if they do not have that high level of consciousness to observe it. Differences, in understanding the reality of the world, create a social disparity between those that have knowledge and awareness as compared to those that are ignorant of it. It creates hurdles in communicating and transmitting ideas. A society that is backward in its awareness of the reality of matter will also be backward in its utility. It will not be able to command materials for the betterment of its members.

Prevalent thinking in the theory of evolution is that the mutation of genes happens to improve the species or create new species that have physically different characteristics. There is one significant flaw in this theory. What about the evolution of a consciousness that is different from the other? Let me try to explain this point. The consciousness of a lion will be different from, let's say, from a Zebra because these are two different creatures with their own culture and personalities. Another question would be whether the consciousness of one lion will be different from the other. A common perception is that they are the same, but scientists have experienced differences in personalities. Quran suggests that each creature will experience death and accountability in the afterlife.

Now consider that an object is observed by an animal and experience the reality of that object. When we look at the theory of evolution, like humans, other species should be interested in improving their lives through manipulation of their environment or developing tools so that they are fittest to survive. But it seems that other animals, except humans, are not interested in doing that in terms of their existence. For instance, a car has no meaning or utility for an animal. Or any other tool that is created by us. These other creatures can see these tools, but we do not know how they perceive them.

The reason for animals' lack of interest in their environment, in my view, is that the theory of evolution assumes that species are not in their perfect state and want to evolve continuously to change. But this could be a mistaken assumption, and the answer could be that an animal has complete knowledge of its existence and does not have any further need to fulfill. Here I am not talking about minor variations to deal with change in the climate and geography. All the other creatures are fully cognizant of their morality and the role they have to play in nature. A bee does not create a different home for itself and is comfortable with the beehive that it develops for her habitation. I am not proposing that the evolution of species might not have occurred through mutation of genes, but that it is not just because of the survival of the fittest. Even Charles Darwin accepts that when he wrote that " Natural Selection has been the main but not exclusive means of modification". Evolution serves a higher purpose that gives rise to new realities that are needed as the universe unfolds itself. The development of a new species is not just the evolution of new body types through mutation of genes but also the rise of a new consciousness. A lion is consciously different from a zebra. The theory of evolution has not considered that. A man, on the other hand, is still exploring his consciousness and has not attained the full potential of it. This evolution of consciousness creates more needs to be satisfied because of a new appreciation of reality. We did not feel the need to have smartphones just 30 years ago, but now once we acquired the knowledge, hardly anyone can imagine living without it.

Another challenge we have to address is that everything in the universe experience decay. There is nothing that stays the same. The reality of an object we perceive now is not the same a little while later. The things around us have no fixed reality at all, just appearances that become part of that moment and are going with it. The reality around us is wasting away to reach a definite destiny. This continuous physical change, which correlates, suggests that the absolute reality is not individual but linked with everything. It means that instead of standalone realities there is one absolute reality from which all these emanate. Philosophers called it the first cause, and religionists call it God.

There is another dimension of reality that we still do not understand. Are the scenes we see in our dreams real or fiction? If they are not real, then why do we have physical changes in our bodies when we experience it? Why does our blood pressure rise, and we sweat while we experience a sensational dream. The Quran suggests that dreams are substantive and a mode of communication.

Dreams are one area of reality about which our knowledge is still in the early stages of exploration. A key question in this regard is how we can have a sensual experience in a dream when our senses are asleep. In an earlier chapter, I suggested that preconception is a priori. Images in a dream that we have never seen before are per-stored in the memory. It means that senses are helpful to bring to our consciousness, from subconscious, ideas, and perceptions related to the physical world rather than these ideas being created for the first time when we experience it. We will discuss this in greater detail in the chapter on dreams.

Another challenge is that there is a reality that is not observed by our senses, so we are unaware of it. Can we say that the truth that is not in our awareness is not significant for our existence or evolution of our consciousness? It means that our ability to know the absolute reality is beyond our physical capability because of the limitations of our senses, or in other words, we have to rely on some other faculties to understand it. Theologians suggest a person has to rely on spiritual enlightenment to attain access to absolute reality. The Quran suggests that revelations enabled humanity to uplift its consciousness. Without this divine intervention, it would be impossible for humanity to embark on a journey of understanding the mysteries of the universe.

I do not know how else to explain the reality of this life. But when I think of it, I visualize Gotham Buddha when he stood up smiling from under the banyan tree after many years of meditation and went to the city to lead a life of a common man.

* * *

Relying on Sights and Sounds

I have always been fascinated by the question of how we see objects. It can help us understand reality. In pursuit of it, I completed an online full credit course offered by a major university to understand it. If you ask doctors, they explain the function of eye from the toolbox of their profession that the light enters the lens, forms an image on the retina, and sends an electrical signal to the brain through the optical nerve. But how does the mind conceive what eyes see? That is where the conversation comes to a deadlock. Before we tackle this paradox, imagine a camera photo that organizes information in a manner that can be perceived by our brain as a comprehensible object. In this scenario, there is no light reflected from an actual object, and entering the eyes, the camera uses color pixels to create an image, or in other words, it is a collage of colors. It is a deception rather than an object.

A philosophical answer will be that when we see an object, say an apple, then the faculty of language that is naming things and our ability to store images work together to form a perception of an idea that is an apple. But where do we store information in the body? Is it the brain? We have so far not been able to locate exactly where the memory is stored and how does the brain process that information as an organ. Scientists have found that long term memory is stored throughout the brain because a specific group of neurons fires up when we observe a similar object. What triggers all these neurons to fire up at the sight of an object? From their normal state before seeing it. These are the questions that need to be explored before we can fully understand how we see things.

In an earlier chapter, we discussed that although intellect is an 'a priori', perception is unique to each person because it emerges from their consciousness built from life experiences. It is, for this reason, it is hard to develop an education curriculum that has uniform results in terms of learning and understanding concepts. The first thing a child learns is to associate hand gestures with sounds and images. Remember the time when you pointed a finger to an object, for example, a chair, and repeated 100 times the name of that object to help a child memorize it. But regardless of how many times you repeat the word, can a child perceive an object if it is not already available in his repertoire of memory? The chair in a room is not just an isolated object, but it has associations with other objects in the environment around it. These associations cannot form without prior knowledge the child has about the object chair, and the process of learning involves exploring these relationships between objects.

It is the dilemma of autistic children that they cannot form these associations as naturally as compared to a child that does not have that condition. We know scientists suggest specific neurons of the brain light up when a person sees an object. Why would that happen to a child who has not seen that object? It is not possible, unless there is already per-existing information about the object in the dormant consciousness of the mind of the child. The process of seeing it for the first time enables us to move it from unconscious to conscious state.

I am proposing that knowledge of our universe is an 'a priori' applicable to all of us, but it is hidden until explored. A conscious layer of individual perceptions is built from it using the unique experience and history of a person. Generally, all humans are born equal in terms of the endowment of intellectual faculties but embark on different paths of self-actualization. A child is born with a consciousness fully loaded with information about concepts and ideas. The purpose of educating is to give him exposure to as many of these ideas as possible so that he can use them when applying thought. A child that has not attended school is not exposed to many ideas, as compared to the one that has that advantage. The birth of a child is also the birth of a consciousness that commences its unique journey of perceptions. The capabilities may be the same, but the accident of birth makes it unequal as the cultural and social condition of the parents plays a significant role. A child born to poor parents is disadvantaged in having sufficient resources.

Let us imagine a situation in which a child does not have the facility of a loving parent or anyone else to guide him. He is all by himself, and no one else is available to mentor his perceptions of the world. In that environment, growing alone, when a child looks at an object, for example, a chair, what does he understand from it. Will the child grow up and discover that this object is to sit on it? Will he use it for some other purpose? Also, will this child be able to assign a name to an object? To develop the faculty of language, without help from an outside agent. The perception of this child will be entirely different from a child that grew up with the help of parents and teachers. In a way, we can say that this difference in perception based on environmental differences is the foundation stone of culture in human society giving rise to class divine of haves and have nots. That does not mean that the intellect of the two children will be superior to or inferior to each other but that they will have a different way of perceiving the reality around them.

Vision and hearing are two senses that aid the formation of perception much more than the other three. Hearing a conversation or viewing a scene helps us form a concept that is much closer to reality than just smelling, tasting, or touching. Language is an area where these two capabilities interact to form one whole. Reading a language is a visual act while listening to it is a hearing act, and the objective of both is to help us develop a perception. It raises another challenge that is when we hear the word chair, it may light up a different part of the brain but create the same perception as when we see a chair or read the word chair. So, a sound, an object, and a symbol should represent the same perception but invoke a different cognitive process in our mind. Perception is not purely a rational event but has an emotional component to it as well. That makes it challenging for the communication of ideas using language through sensory methods of sound or written word. It is difficult to resolve this paradox unless the absolute reality of the objects is known to those involved in communication using a perfect medium that does not have flaws. We do not yet have access to that perfect medium.

Now imagine an animal, for example, a dog that sees a chair. What happens in the animal consciousness? The mechanics are the same as humans, that the rays of light form an image on the retina and optic nerve sending signals to the brain. But that is where probably the similarity with humans ends. There could be two possibilities. First that an animal has the same perception of objects as humans, but the intellectual capability lacks cognitive power to associate it with other things to find utility for it. Second could be that animals have a different perception of objects than humans. We do not know how animals name objects and use their cognitive faculties to understand their association with other items in the environment. Our knowledge of the animal mind is limited right now. But the notion that animals do not have intelligence is mistaken, and slowly it is emerging that they do have it, but we do not understand it yet. The Quran sheds some light on this and proposes that animals not just have intelligence, but also the faculty of language. Here are the verses related to the story of ants narrated by the Quran:

Chapter 27 Verses 16 - 27: And Solomon was David's heir. He said: "O ye people! We have been taught the speech of birds, and on us has been bestowed (a little) of all things: this is indeed Grace manifest (from Allah.)". And before Solomon were marshaled his hosts,- of Jinns and men and birds, and they were all kept in order and ranks. At length, when they came to a (lowly) valley of ants, one of the ants said: "O ye ants, get into your habitations, lest Solomon and his hosts crush you (under foot) without knowing it." And he took a muster of the Birds; and he said: "Why is it I see not the Hoopoe? Or is he among the absentees? "I will certainly punish him with a severe penalty, or execute him, unless he bring me a clear reason (for absence)." But the Hoopoe tarried not far: he (came up and) said: "I have compassed (territory) which thou hast not compassed, and I have come to thee from Saba with tidings true. "I found (there) a woman ruling over them and provided with every requisite; and she has a magnificent throne. "I found her and her people worshipping the sun besides Allah: Satan has made their deeds seem pleasing in their eyes, and has kept them away from the Path,- so they receive no guidance,-

"(Kept them away from the Path), that they should not worship Allah, Who brings to light what is hidden in the heavens and the earth, and knows what ye hide and what ye reveal. "Allah!- there is no god but He!- Lord of the Throne Supreme!" (Solomon) said: "Soon shall we see whether thou hast told the truth or lied!

Many insightful lessons can be deducted from the above story that can guide our inquiry. It suggests that insects and animals have a language through which they communicate. They have consciousness of their environment as well as the intelligence to analyze and form opinions of danger or safety. They have emotions of fear and concern for each other. It also suggests that humans can understand animal communication. An interesting point to note that Prophet Sulaiman (AS) suggested that animals can lie as well in these verses of Chapter 27 that is a cognitive function and requires intellect as well as a free will. British Broadcasting Corporation (BBC), a while back, broadcast a documentary (reference section has the links) on animal intelligence. Scientists found that some birds were able to solve complex problems as well as the ability of Elephants to have memory and expression of grief at the loss of a family member. They found that whales can communicate over long distances as well as dolphin ability to seek pleasure through play.

To understand animal behavior, we have to explore whether they have a concept of good and evil or is it something just related to human condition only. We cannot know an answer to this until we start developing the science of animal psychology, about which our knowledge is still quite basic. One main hurdle to overcome this hurdle will be to learn the language of animals so that we can have conversations with them. It was the art of communication that enabled psychologists to develop their science of human psychology. Until a person speaks, we cannot tell their mental condition. The incoherence of speech is the first sign of a mental disorder. By narrating the above story of Prophet Sulaiman (AS), the Quran suggests that men can have a conversation with animals. An orthodox approach would be to consider it a miracle and hence beyond the reach of humans or try to explore ways to see if that knowledge is within our grasp. I will support the latter rather than the former.

Now let us reconsider the scenario mentioned previously, that an object is observed by both a human and an animal. Will they have the same experience of reality? The absolute nature of an object should be the same for all consciousness living in the world. The point is that our reliance on human consciousness alone in understanding the world around us is limiting our knowledge. We need to find ways to understand animal consciousness and incorporate that in our perception of reality. That will help us have a better understanding of reality and help us achieve our self-actualization.

We all know that computers can share not only memory, using Bluetooth, for instance, but processing power as well. Another question that scientists should explore: Is it possible for one person to have access to the memory or brainpower of another person? Here I am not talking about brain transplants rather one organ shared by two people at the same time. It will help us learn whether sharing the same organ brain translates into the same mind or a different mind that is unique to each person. It will be a step towards finding the soul.

* * *

Tasting the Consciousness

It is fascinating the way senses tickle our consciousness that makes life on earth interesting. Continuing our discussion about the way we see, hear, taste, smell, and touch objects around us raises in us an awareness of a life that we cannot say for sure whether it is real or fictional. Previously we tried to address perception through sight and sound, we should now look at how do we taste things? We will look at this question from scientific, evolutionary, pantheistic, metaphysical, and finally, from a religious point of view. It will not be an exhaustive presentation, but I expect it will be sufficient to force you to think.

Cursory research helps us learn that scientifically there are 2000-4000 taste buds located on the tongue. Each taste bud has 10-50 sensory cells that are regenerated every week. Scientists classify taste into five basic categories that are sweet, sour, salty, bitter, and savory (also called umami). According to scientists, these tastes are sensed by the sensory cells because of a chemical reaction produced by various enzymes, in our saliva, produced in the mouth when they interact with food.

Let us consider an example so that we can build our understanding through it. Imagine you are eating food that has salt in it. Salt is composed of two chemical elements Sodium (chemical symbol Na) and Chlorine (Chemical symbol Cl). Each salt molecule is one atom each of Sodium and Chlorine represented by the chemical formula NaCl. As soon as the food gets in touch with our tongue, we can tell, almost instantly, there was salt in it. How does this process work?

Scientists will tell you that enzymes in the mouth interact with salt (NaCl), the sensory cell in the taste buds on the tongue send a signal to the brain. But this is where simplicity ends, and complexity starts. How did sensory cells learn to differentiate between various taste signals associated with different food items? When that signal reaches the brain, how does it arrive at the consciousness of salt that we experience? Is the taste part of the molecule of Salt (NaCl), or is the taste in the enzyme that works on salt in the mouth or taste is in the consciousness once it is determined there is the presence of salt in food? These are substantive questions because scientifically, all taste buds can do is to send a signal to the brain verifying the presence and quantity of salt in the food. The sensation of taste is not their concern. It is these questions that we have to now look at from an evolutionary, metaphysical, and religious point of view because the understanding of science is still at a very early stage.

From the evolutionary perspective, senses have a utilitarian purpose. It suggests that we evolved senses to protect us from harm so that we can survive and continue as a species, remember the survival of the fittest. To elaborate on this point, the sense of taste protects us from consuming too much of any substance, say salt or sugar, that could be harmful to our body. This approach does not provide all the answers because there is a certain level of artistic and cultural aspect of the sensation of salt with which evolution should not concern itself. Secondly, how did the consciousness of taste of salt arouse for the first time from not being present beforehand? In other words, how does that particular sensation we feel arose when the salt first touched the taste bud. At that moment of the first instance, the bud should have just sent a signal to the brain. How and why the brain developed a particular sensation that had a peculiar artistic and cultural aspect to it. The theory of evolution fails to provide answers to these questions.

Another challenge is to find out if the consciousness of taste is similar in other living beings based on the theory of evolution. If evolution worked similarly on all species, the sensation of tasting should be comparable. The physical needs of each creature in terms of quantity of nutritional chemicals, like salt, could be unique, but the sensation of it as a taste has to be the same, especially if it is in the essence of the compound. Since the compound is unchanging, one way to understand differences in taste can be through the study of enzymes, structure of taste buds, and brain. Science cannot verify it with certainty because we still do not know how the animal sensation of taste works.

A pantheist would suggest that art and culture are part of nature. An association of these with the sensation of taste, developed in the consciousness during evolution. It still fails to confirm whether the sensation of taste is part of the chemical compound, enzymes that work on it, or consciousness that perceives it. It also does not provide an answer to how did it arose the first time in the consciousness or became part of nature. The bottom line, it does not provide definitive answers to the existence of awareness of taste.

Now let us look at it from a religious perspective. The Quran narrates the story of the creation of Adam in many chapters.

Chapter 2 Verses 30 – 32: Behold, thy Lord said to the angels: "I will create a vicegerent on earth." They said: "Wilt Thou place therein one who will make mischief therein and shed blood?- whilst we do celebrate Thy praises and glorify Thy holy (name)?" He said: "I know what ye know not." And He taught Adam the names of all things; then He placed them before the angels, and said: "Tell me the names of these if ye are right." They said: "Glory to Thee, of knowledge We have none, save what Thou Hast taught us: In truth it is Thou Who art perfect in knowledge and wisdom." He said: "O Adam! Tell them their names." When he had told them, Allah said: "Did I not tell you that I know the secrets of heaven and earth, and I know what ye reveal and what ye conceal?

There are many symbolic messages in that story for us to ponder over. An important point to note is that Adam presented names of things that were not in the knowledge of angels. What could that knowledge be? Now imagine if that knowledge is the emergence of a new consciousness that is unique to men. The awareness of the sensation of salt or taste that only he can feel and express. That sensation is unique to him. It only exists in his being. It is not part of salt, an enzyme that works on it, taste buds that send the signal to the brain, but it is in the consciousness that is only for humans. Metaphysically it means that religion suggests that awareness of taste is an a priori. The sensory organs are there to facilitate it.

* * *

Dreams

British philosopher Bertrand Russell made a striking observation about dreams. He suggested that if our dreams were coherent night after night, then it would be difficult for us to differentiate between our living and sleeping moments. I am sure you can imagine the effect such a situation would have on our lives. Dreaming is a fascinating aspect of our lives and still largely a mystery. Why do we experience dreams? Do other species dream too?

We do not know anything about animal dreams, but Sigmund Freud and Carl G. Jung did a lot of research on understanding human dreams. They suggest that it is the interplay of our experiences during a day, our fears, and our curiosity about things that we do not understand. Freud observed many patients and recorded their dream experiences. He presented these findings in the book *Dream Psychology Psychoanalysis for Beginners*. In the book, he made a startling disclosure about creativity. He wrote that "from the communications of some of the most highly productive persons, such as Goethe and Helmholtz, we learn, indeed, that the most essential and original parts in their creations came to them in the form of inspirations and reached their perceptions almost finished". He suggested that those experiences during the daytime are processed by our unconscious mind and presented to us in the dream. Our unfulfilled desires and emotions provide the foundation for these dreams.

Freud did not have the facility of an MRI to observe brain activity associated with seeing unique objects and experiencing emotions. His hypothesis on dreaming is still considered the foundations on which a plausible scientific theory can evolve.

Professor of neuroscience and psychology at UC Berkeley, Dr. Matthew Walker, in his book *Why We Sleep: Unlocking the Power of Sleep and Dreams*, talks about research findings on understanding dreams. He shares the scientific findings that have tried to analyze brain activity during sleep when seeing an object in a dream and compare it with brain activity seeing the same object during daytime. They disagree with Freud that daytime objects play any role as it turns out to be just 1% content of it. But they do agree that 30% of the emotions experienced during daytime were present in a dream. They have also provided insight into the sleep pattern, the state of our brain, during each of these stages. But none of them suggest that we should ignore dreams as frivolous.

When we sleep, every night, we experience multiple cycles of REM-sleep (rapid eye movement sleep) and NREM-sleep (non-rapid eye movement sleep). During the NREM-sleep cycle, the heart rate goes down, bone and muscles grow, the repairs are performed, and immunity replenished. REM-sleep is the cycle when we experience high emotions, and it is usually in this cycle that we experience dreams. Dr. Walker suggests that dreaming during the REM-Sleep helps us repair our emotional self. Our dreams portray those emotions that we have experienced during the day but remain unaddressed. Dreams help us deal with these unresolved emotions and maintain mental health. Psychologists propose effective dreams should not have a link with our memory but rather detached from it. If they are not detached from it, as experienced by patients with post-traumatic distress disorder (PTSD), we experience a nightmare that disrupts and causes damage to our sleep. It results in sleep deprivation that causes many other injuries, including but not limited to a lack of empathy and the onset of depression. A good night's sleep with pleasant dreams does play a role in our health.

Dr. Walker proposes that the REM-sleep dream serves another important function that is to help us perform intelligent problem solving and creativity.

To illustrate the creative function of dreaming, he provides many examples, for example, Dimitri Mendeleev who solved the puzzle of the chemical periodic table in a dream. It matches the experience of Goethe and Helmholtz presented by Freud. Dr. Matthew then designed a laboratory experiment to confirm that REM-sleep dreaming induces creativity. His experiments verified that the problem-solving capability increased by 30-35% during REM-sleep dream cycle. He also observed that problem solving, in the middle of a REM-sleep dream cycle is much different when compared to daytime while awake.

He postulates that the creativity and problem solving in REM-sleep is an interplay of active dreaming and associated content available in the conscious gathered by the person researching an issue. That produces distant connections between data points that are not visible in the waking moment. Relational memory processing gets a boost from REM-sleep dreaming. It helps in comprehending what was unresolved in a daytime contemplation. REM-sleep dream requires help from past experiences to be able to help us solve complex problems and develop abstract creative ideas. It also confirms our earlier proposition that we are born with a mind full of a priori knowledge that is in our subconscious. We have to uncover that knowledge through a deliberate effort throughout our lives. All we are doing in a dream is to use that knowledge hidden in the unconscious and associate it with new facts gathered to reveal some hitherto hidden knowledge of our mind.

Dr. Walker suggests that a child, barely 18 months old, uses this creative function of REM-sleep dream comprehension to sort complex grammar rules much earlier than they learn it in a school. It confirms our proposition in an earlier chapter that intellect is endowed with faculty of language as an 'a priori' because only then can rules be understood using the creative function of the unconscious in a dream. He speculates that toddlers need a long duration of that REM-sleep dreaming to process the data gathered to develop their intellectual faculty. Axiom sleep over it, he advises, has benefits.

Our dreams appear to be irrational and random. In it, we experience ourselves possessing supernatural powers traversing vast distances in the flash of a second. We also experience trauma, physical injury, emotional crisis, and even death in our dreams. That makes us anxious to understand the meaning of all this. Psychologists, so far, are not convinced that dreams have any deeper meaning or contain messages about some future events. Freud concluded his book with these words:

"And How about the value of the dream for knowledge of the future? That, of course, we cannot consider. One feel inclined to substitute: 'for knowledge of the past'. For the dream originates from the past in every sense. To be sure, the ancient belief that the dream reveals the future is not entirely devoid of truth. By representing to us a wish as fulfilled the dream certainly leads us into the future; but this future, taken by the dreamer as present, has been formed into the likeness of that passed by the indestructible wish".

Science is trying to understand the mechanics of the dream, but it does not fully understand it yet. Many unexplained phenomena are surrounding it. If we are sleeping, who is seeing the dream? What is the entity that is experiencing this jumbled and disorderly consciousness? Religion explains dreams differently. It is considered a communication from another domain that sometimes contains messages that can help us improve our lives or solve an issue. It suggests that dreams convey knowledge of the future. Following verses narrate the story of Prophet Yousuf's (Joseph) interpretation of dreams:

Chapter 8 Verse 43: Remember in thy dream Allah showed them to thee as few: if He had shown them to thee as many, ye would surely have been discouraged, and ye would surely have disputed in (your) decision; but Allah saved (you): for He knoweth well the (secrets) of (all) hearts.

Chapter 12 Verse 4-6: Behold! Joseph said to his father: "O my father! I did see eleven stars and the sun and the moon: I saw them prostrate themselves to me!" Said (the father): "My (dear) little son! relate not thy vision to thy brothers, lest they concoct a plot against thee: for Satan is to man an avowed enemy! "Thus will thy Lord choose thee and teach thee the interpretation of stories (and events) and perfect His favour to thee and to the posterity of Jacob - even as He perfected it to thy fathers Abraham and Isaac aforetime! for Allah is full of knowledge and wisdom."

Chapter 12 Verse 36-37: Now with him there came into the prison two young men. Said one of them: "I see myself (in a dream) pressing wine." said the other: "I see myself (in a dream) carrying bread on my head, and birds are eating, thereof." "Tell us" (they said) "The truth and meaning thereof: for we see thou art one that doth good (to all)." He said: "Before any food comes (in due course) to feed either of you, I will surely reveal to you the truth and meaning of this ere it befall you: that is part of the (duty) which my Lord hath taught me. I have (I assure you) abandoned the ways of a people that believe not in Allah and that (even) deny the Hereafter.

Chapter 12 Verse 40-41: "O my two companions of the prison! As to one of you, he will pour out the wine for his lord to drink: as for the other, he will hang from the cross, and the birds will eat from off his head. (so) hath been decreed that matter whereof ye twain do enquire"...

Chapter 12 Verse 43-49: The king (of Egypt) said: "I do see (in a vision) seven fat kine, whom seven lean ones devour, and seven green ears of corn, and seven (others) withered. O ye chiefs! Expound to me my vision if it be that ye can interpret visions." They said: "A confused medley of dreams: and we are not skilled in the interpretation of dreams." But the man who had been released, one of the two (who had been in prison) and who now bethought him after (so long) a space of time, said: "I will tell you the truth of its interpretation: send ye me (therefore)." "O Joseph!" (he said) "O man of truth! Expound to us (the dream) of seven fat kine whom seven lean ones devour, and of seven green ears of corn and (seven) others withered: that I may return to the people, and that they may understand." (Joseph) said: "For seven years shall ye diligently sow as is your wont: and the harvests that ye reap, ye shall leave them in the ear,- except a little, of which ye shall eat. "Then will come after that (period) seven dreadful (years), which will devour what ye shall have laid by in advance for them,- (all) except a little which ye shall have (specially) guarded. Then will come after that (period) a year in which the people will have abundant water, and in which they will press (wine and oil)."

The dream of Prophet Ibrahim (AS) is narrated in the following verses:

Chapter 37 Verses 100-109: "O my Lord! Grant me a righteous (son)!"So We gave him the good news of a boy ready to suffer and forbear.And when he attained to working with him, he said: O my son! surely I have seen in a dream that I should sacrifice you; consider then what you see. He said: O my father! do what you are commanded; if Allah please, you will find me of the patient ones.So when they had both submitted their wills (to Allah), and he had laid him prostrate on his forehead (for sacrifice),We called out to him "O Abraham!"Thou hast already fulfilled the vision!" - thus indeed do We reward those who do right.For this was obviously a trial-And We ransomed him with a momentous sacrifice:And We left (this blessing) for him among generations (to come) in later times:"Peace and salutation to Abraham!"Thus do We reward the doers of good.Surely he was one of Our believing servants.And We gave him the good news of Ishaq, a prophet among the good ones.

The above stories of Prophets Yousuf (AS) and Ibrahim (AS) suggest that dreams have meaning. One common feature for an extraordinary but meaningful dream is that it repeats for many days with the same contents and details to get the attention of the person. The Qurans' message from the dream of Ibrahim (Abraham) is that God ultimately did not want a human sacrifice. The question then is, why would God choose to have this test of a possible human sacrifice? I have struggled with this question for a long time and do not have a definite answer. One explanation that comes to my mind, but that requires separate scholarly research, is that there was a tradition of human sacrifice in many pagan religions around the world. God had to demonstrate to humanity that He do not seek human sacrifice and used Prophet Ibrahim (AS) to teach that lesson.

* * *

Language

Throughout this book, we have referred to the faculty of language and briefly touched upon the subject as well. From the above discussion, it is clear, the growth of consciousness in any individual depends on the use of language, especially in our social interactions. It is also the medium for the transmission of knowledge to the next generation as we raise our children. We have an emotional association with words because if it was devoid of it, then it could not be used by a novelist as a medium for a work of art that is fictional, not factual. This makes it imperative for us to look at the evolution of this profound human enterprise. From the evolutionary perspective, there is a difference of just a few genes between an ape and a human. But the difference in the use of language, art, and culture is exponential, at least from our perspective. Another observation is the existence of diversity and a variety of dialects developed by humanity. While humanity practices this diverse tool, there is no evidence that apes of Africa have a different language than apes of America or Asia.

An evolutionist would say that over millions of years, the human species has developed this faculty. The problem is that we have yet to find evidence of a community where some form of language was nonexistent. Another challenge is how this faculty evolved. Philosophers Adam Smith and Nam Chomsky presented their theories on the origin of language faculty in humans. They attribute it to a chance mutation that produced an almost overnight ability to have a language. Apart from that, many theories explain the process of evolution of dialects like bow-wow and pooh-pooh. This sounds funny but these are actual theories. Bow-wow theory suggests that humans started giving names to things based on the sounds generated by objects, animals, and birds. The pooh-pooh theory, on the other hand, suggests that names were given to things not based on the sounds they produced but independent of it. In other words, it was a more artistic rendering of the world around us. Even if we can understand the construction of names, there is still no definitive answer available about the evolution of grammar that plays a very critical part in language. For instance, when we say the apple is sweet. It is easy to understand apple was a name given to an object, and word sweet is a name associated with a sensation. But how and why did we develop the articles is, are, etc.? As well as the rules to use it. For a community to adopt this practice, it would require consensus on grammar rules because communication involves more than one person. Now consider that there is not one, but thousands of dialects used around the world. Each one as complex as the other.

Another challenge is that the complexity of the language is unique to a human. Other species seem to have been lagging significantly, although they have been in existence longer than humans. It does not mean animals do not have language faculty but that they do not preserve and convey ideas, for instance, by writing a book or recording audio. Man, transfer knowledge to the next generation through language while an animal does it through genes, training, and experimentation only. Man conveys thoughts, ideas, and data to others without coming into physical contact with them through books, but animals require physical interaction to do that and have never written a book. At least, we have not discovered one so far. Their ability to transmit knowledge to the next generation is through genes. Also, animals do not seem to use language for the discovery and development of new technologies and tools. There is no apparent desire in them to improve their lives. There seems to be no answer to these wide differences in language faculty between species when the comparison is made with humans and other animals. It adds to the complexity of the question.

Let us now consider the story of Adam (AS) when logos were granted to him by God in which language was it or was it just the ability to assign names to objects and form associations between them that give rise to many different dialects, and cultures. Another thing to consider is what language was used by angels to converse with God or was it just inspiration rather than the actual utterance of words. The religious story of Adam can be denied by science by proving that at a particular point in the process of evolution, humans did not use language. So far, there is no evidence that the ability to use language was ever absent in the human species.

The point is that the ability to produce a language is hardwired in the human gene or nature. Since we want to use scientific evidence, let me again use the example of a computer whose operating system is developed based on the programming language c++. This operating system gives the computer machine the ability to help us to write a letter to our boss or family in plain English language. It would not be possible if the ability to produce language was not present on the computer. The same is true about humans, and the Quranic story of Adam is to convey that.

Now imagine that the ability to produce communication was limited to only one language. That would be terrible because it was the diversity of dialects that added to the diversity and richness of human art and quality of life. Imagine jazz in Urdu language or Urdu ghazal singing in English that are two genres of music practiced in the West and South Asia respectively.

God says that the command of the universe was given to men (Chapter

33 Verse 72: *We did indeed offer the Trust to the Heavens and the Earth and the Mountains; but they refused to undertake it, being afraid thereof: but man undertook it;- He was indeed unjust and foolish;-).* To take command and control of something can't be possible without knowing its nature. And an expression of this nature requires the ability to speak or present ideas to others. So, in a way, language is the ability to convey consciousness of an 'a priori' to another consciousness that should have the same a priori to receive it. In simple English, both the sender and receiver should have the ability to produce language.

The fundamental components in all languages are the same, that is alphabets, words, unique sounds, and rules of grammar to link words together to have a coherent meaning. Audio, or sound, is needed for the oral transmission of language but not for written and vice versa. No language is devoid of these basic building blocks, that means the ability to build a language is present in our intellectual capacity, and a child is born with it.

Another puzzle is how does a child learn grammar to speak sentences without having any knowledge about it from pure gestures or mimicry of parents. In the chapter on dreams, we discussed some theories to solve this puzzle. Within no time, a child is capable of perfectly structured sentences without help from anyone that he has never uttered before. It cannot be possible through memory alone. The first highly intellectual faculty a child develops is spoken language with a perfect sense of grammar and sentence structure. In school also, communication starts from spoken before transitioning to written to facilitate the child to be able to read books to gain knowledge of other sciences.

Which language did first man speak, and that language should be the bases or root of all later dialects? The Quran is silent about it, and there is divine wisdom in it. Or else we would have a master and slave class struggle between races.

Politics, History and Social Development

Secularism and Faith

In the West, modernity is equated with the adoption of secularism as a political philosophy. They believe that this separation of Church and State allowed rationality and tolerance to prevail. This contributed towards advancements in science and technology as well as making their societies prosperous. Interestingly, a secular mind looks at a social problem from a purely rational and mathematical way without giving due consideration to human emotions, culture, and religion that play a role in defining the attitudes and motivation of the people. This simplistic approach to human relationships and interactions creates an unreal dynamic that may work for a time but ultimately produces a stalemate and deadlock. The social and political crisis faced around the world is the failure of secularism to contain greed of the capitalist and rising discontent with the existing liberal democratic order. People believe that politicians serve the vested interests of multinational corporations and the military establishment.

People of faith will suggest that a human, by its very nature, is a rebel when it comes to obeying divine instruction, and this separation of the Church from the State is nothing but another form of it. The story of Adam (AS) sheds light on this rebellious nature when he ignored divine instruction and tasted from the forbidden tree. This attitude to rebel continues until today in one form or the other just like secularism wants to have independence from divine influence around politics and economy. In the secular realm, politics is about gaining power for the worldly desires of the community and the satisfaction of individual egos of those in power. In Islam, politics is not just about serving the community. It is also about pleasing God and seeking a reward in the hereafter for good works. It offers an incentive for good behavior rather than treating it as an indifferent compulsion.

Secularists claim that they are not against God, faith, and religion by allowing people to practice it in their private domain. It creates a contradiction in their political and personal life. They do not have to be inspired in political decisions by their faith in God. Secularism demands voluntary divorce of religion when a person is engaged in politics that is almost impossible to achieve. This anomaly is the Achilles heel of secularism and will ultimately become the reason for its failure.

The discipline of political science is trying to contain the emotional aspect in politics because, as a science, it promotes rationalism and rejects everything that is irrational and cannot be measured. God is one of those emotional, hence irrational, ideas that are unacceptable to political science. In this, it supposes that the knowledge of human psychology and relations is now complete. If it was not, then it cannot be sure that its recipes for managing society will work.

Secularists consider religion as a divider of society and the foundation of intolerance in a community. The reality is that intolerance, like many other attributes, is a human condition. It is part of our basic instinct to survive and rely more on those with whom we have some social affinity. Blaming religion as a source of division and intolerance is a secularist's reason to promote the idea that God does not have a role to play in society and should be relegated to the private life of individuals.

God is comfortable with his creatures pursuing different religions, evident from a plethora of faiths. God is leaving the question of faith in Him for the afterlife. He does not withhold his blessings from those that do not believe in Him. Based on this evidence, blaming religion for intolerance can be classified more as the narrowness of humanity itself and its incapacity to deal with matters of a diversity of faith. If secularism does not want to have communal divisions, then there should be no political parties as well because they cause these divisions based on their ideological approach to dealing with social issues. There are social groups based on the ideology of right and left that have nothing to do with religion. Secularists accept that pursuing one unifying ideology is not in the human condition, but they are still artificially trying to separate faith from the community. It has never worked throughout history. Majorities need to be sensitive to minorities, and differences in faith do not and should not hamper our human affinity towards each other.

As discussed in the previous chapter on religion and dogma, it is not religion that promotes ideas of violence but dogma that cannot be allowed to dictate terms in a state. Dogma should be treated differently from religion and is usually the cause of division in society. Religion is pursued by an individual to have spiritual elevation to realize self-actualization. Dogma is a collective pursuit that has cultural and tribal aspects to it.

A more viable model for secularism and religion to work together is to look at the higher-level ideals. A state is not the preacher or promoter of a particular dogma pursued by a sect but rather upholder of higher moral values that are important for the realization of human potential. These higher values are freedom of expression, religion, assembly, and choice of a career. When we call a country by a specific religious connotation like the Islamic Republic of Pakistan or Christian Democrats Union (CDU) of Germany, it does not mean people of other religions cannot be members of the community but that the majority pursue Islamic tradition. It also does not mean that the State has the right to interfere in the religious practices of individuals and demand adopting a preferred dogma. It only means that states pursue the moral and social code presented by a particular religion.

The Secularist view that God is indifferent to the affairs of humanity is also not compatible with the idea of God. God has designed men to be social animals. To consider that He will remain unconcerned about social behavior of humanity is misleading. Histories of prophets and the revelations sent to them include guidance about the affairs of society is a clear indication that men need advice in spheres of life. The advantage Islam has over other revealed religions is that the revelations are still available in the original format that can provide the world guidance in these matters. It is a mistaken and misguided notion that the Quran promotes violence or has contradictions in it. Contradictions appear when verses of the Quran are quoted out of context.

Secularism suggests that it is not the concern of the State to worry about the spiritual while bodily needs like education, health, and safety are its responsibility. But this approach does not take into account that there has never been a time in human history when the idea of God or religion was not present. Religion has always been an integral and inseparable component of human existence and has to be taken into consideration in organizing a society.

The idea of social capitalism is borrowed from religion. In a purely secular society where capitalism dominates, there should be no concern for the suffering of other human beings. It would be irrational to spend your hard-earned money on another person without a reward for it. It is the religion that provides a rational base for charity by suggesting that there is a reward in the afterlife. In the absence of this idea, there would be chaos and conflict arising from disincentive to help others. Islam proposes that income equality is part of the social order, and it is incumbent upon those with wealth to take care of their disadvantaged neighbors, relatives, and city dwellers. Their failure to discharge this responsibility could subject them to accountability in the afterlife.

Even in the implementation of the rule of law and justice, religion comes to the aid of the secularists. A human judge cannot guarantee that he will be right 100% of the time. A community may have a good judicial system, but the chance of human error in deciding a case creates anxiety. This anxiety is alleviated by religion guaranteeing that there could be recourse for injustice in the afterlife. The absence of this sense of an overlord that has the power not to overlook even the slightest injustice and abuse, keeps all of us sane and hopeful. Hopelessness can be fatal for a community.

The bottom line is that God's involvement in the affairs of men is a blessing. Without it, society will descend into disarray and chaos. Islam is the most modern religion and does not separate the interests of the collective from the individual. As secularism lays down on the sickbed, Islam will provide answers to the social crisis faced by the world. Will Muslims lead this renaissance or not should be of real concern to us.

* * *

Politics and Human Nature

Consider a person living all by himself. In that state, he would be free, and not inhibited by the opinions and views of another person when he engages in an activity, for instance, building a home on a particular parcel of land or hunting for food. It raises the question of whether in that situation, the conscience will be dormant as there is no probability of committing a sin or engaging in crime that could impinge on the rights of another. It also raises another question what would Satan or Iblis be doing? What kind of sins, he would be suggesting to this lone man? Or does there have to be a pair to have the potency to commit sin? We must not forget that Adam was not alone in heaven when he was instigated by evil to eat from the forbidden tree. This desire to be associated with others suggests that living in a community is hardwired into the human psyche, and they cannot function outside it. It is for this reason probably that solitary confinement is so overbearing for inmates and is considered inhuman punishment.

Let us take this discussion a step further and add a woman to the equation. Now a single couple is living by themselves in one corner of the world. Will there be an element of politics between them to negotiate terms of life, or they live in harmony complementing the needs of each other. There might be discussions on the type of meal to cook or to participate in entertainment activities. Although the individual liberties of the two will be curtailed to some extent. There is no conflict of interest between them.

Let us suppose that instead of a woman, there is a man added to the equation. So, two men are living in a secluded place. In that case, there will be some conflict of interest as the psychological and physiological makeup of the two is similar and that creates conflict as their needs are the same. Let us here refer the story of sons of Adam, Qabil (Cane) and Habil (Abel) narrated in Quran:

Chapter 5 Verses 27 – 30: Recite to them the truth of the story of the two sons of Adam. Behold! they each presented a sacrifice (to Allah): It was accepted from one, but not from the other. Said the latter: "Be sure I will slay thee." "Surely," said the former, "Allah doth accept of the sacrifice of those who are righteous. "If thou dost stretch thy hand against me, to slay me, it is not for me to stretch my hand against thee to slay thee: for I do fear Allah, the cherisher of the worlds. "For me, I intend to let thee draw on thyself my sin as well as thine, for thou wilt be among the companions of the fire, and that is the reward of those who do wrong." The (selfish) soul of the other led him to the murder of his brother: he murdered him, and became (himself) one of the lost ones.

Bible narrate the same story in Genesis 4.1 – 4.8: Adam made love to his wife Eve, and she became pregnant and gave birth to Cain. She said, "With the help of the Lord I have brought forth a man." Later she gave birth to his brother Abel.

Now Abel kept flocks, and Cain worked the soil. In the course of time Cain brought some of the fruits of the soil as an offering to the Lord.And Abel also brought an offering—fat portions from some of the firstborn of his flock. The Lord looked with favor on Abel and his offering, 5but on Cain and his offering he did not look with favor. So Cain was very angry, and his face was downcast.

Then the Lord said to Cain, "Why are you angry? Why is your face downcast? If you do what is right, will you not be accepted? But if you do not do what is right, sin is crouching at your door; it desires to have you, but you must rule over it."

Now Cain said to his brother Abel, "Let's go out to the field." While they were in the field, Cain attacked his brother Abel and killed him.

Now let's imagine another scenario in which there are two men and a woman or vice versa. In that scenario, there is bound to be competition, conflict of interest, and a change in behavior. The two men will compete for the attention of the woman for procreation. The woman will have more choice in deciding a mate. The person that loses the woman also loses the ability to continue his lineage. It raises the stakes as the person that loses out when children are born and his share in votes and production decline. The other solution could be that men share the woman, but then who would have the first right. Rules have to be devised as a woman or newborn could die giving birth to the child of the man who earns the second right to mate while giving birth to the child of the first to mate. Financial and economic interests are other dimensions to be considered in the above examples because of the death and appropriation of property among living inheritors. These situations became the founding premise for the emergence of politics, that is to devise rules that create some balance between these competing interests in a group. In the absence of politics, the next option for people is to resort to fighting until death so that only one man and one woman is left. As the numbers grow, into millions, the complexities multiply, the consensus is hard to achieve and requires the introduction of agencies, that is police and courts to resolve the conflicts arising from the interpretation of rules and their application.

Over centuries various systems and concepts were evolved to address these complexities of human society. Many philosophers and thinkers delved into the development of ideas to organize human enterprise harmoniously and efficiently. From a benevolent monarchy to liberal democracy, humanity has tried everything. We have tried all these approaches to develop a better world for ourselves. Ideologies of secularism, capitalism, socialism, and communism were applied to achieve the best social order. Most of these concept's appeal to the rational side of human nature and try to control or ignore the emotional side. For instance, Karl Marx considered that economic interest supersedes all other interests of human endeavor and that reducing income inequalities could solve social issues like poverty and class conflict. He focused on the materialistic impulse of human career to be the defining activity overriding all spheres of collective life. It is a faulty assumption that an artist, for example, is not driven by the greed for compensation to create art. Art is the desire to convey reality uniquely, as experienced by the artist, that was invisible until then. Or to bring an experience of emotions or pain that is shared by all humanity.

Capitalism considers that capabilities and motivations are different in each individual. Every person has the right to maximize his or her economic potential by bringing their innovation to the marketplace. The state should ensure that everyone gets an equal opportunity. The driver of capitalism is greed, while the source of all evil is greed as well in the eyes of Marx. Socialism, on the other hand, authorizes the state to use her coercive power to take away residual income generated by high performing individuals to redistribute it to the poor. It takes away the incentive for the individual to be successful by assuming a higher risk.

In religious terms, Christianity presents humanity to be in a condition of perpetual condemnation resulting from the original sin. All acts in this world should be committed to repaying that original sin so that the person can regain the lost glory and ascend back to the heavens. It was that pessimistic view of life that was not compatible with the capitalistic aspiration of maximizing economic gain and defining happiness in terms of fat bank balance. To resolve this inherent conflict of interest, between religion and politics, a possible way out was to reject the role of religion in the political sphere and relegate it to the status of a subjective practice of an individual to find his salvation. Since a higher understanding of the material world was accomplished, through scientific advancement, it meant the dominance of rational over emotional self. It is now capable of managing its affairs and did not need the irrational ideals of faith to interfere in collective life.

Islam recognizes that human nature is evolutionary, and that each child is born free from any past sin carrying his possibility of a new career. It presents humans to be a combination of both an emotional and rational self. This human is in a constant struggle to attain higher consciousness by exploring the realities hidden in the world around us. Rational is related to the science that is to understand the nature of things, and the emotional is to praise art, culture, and God that created it as the first cause. A unique idea proposed by Islam is that the scientific quest is the quest for God and recognizing Him. It accepts that some will not recognize an omnipotent singular God or reject it altogether, but the mandate to judge these individuals is not the domain of the society and its laws. Islam pushes the human soul forward by challenging the intellect to explore the material and benefit from the bounties offered by it. But at the same time, it advises not to forget the less fortunate and to share the benefits through a voluntary act of charity. It proposes social capitalism whereby profit is not the only motive but also social responsibility.

The politics in Islamic thought are motivated by the humanistic ideals that are freedom of religion, freedom of expression, and respect for other humans. It advises that balance between these competing interests is a constant struggle, and collective effort in the guidance of revelations would make it easier to create social harmony without compromising the spiritual well being.

* * *

Mandate of the Majority

One of the basic building blocks of liberal democracy and the modern nation-state is the sovereignty of the people and the mandate of the majority. It is this mandate that legitimizes a democratic government and grants them the agency to legislate new laws and make executive decisions. It raises two questions with which political scientists are still grappling. First, whether majorities can make the right decision? And second, how to accommodate dissidents that may not have majority support but provide a new direction to the nation? Consider the example of Greens Party (GP) in Germany that wants compliance with laws to protect the environment. But they never got a majority mandate despite offering a manifesto that resonates with people. Before we tackle these questions about majority mandate, let us first briefly review how the concept of adult franchise developed in the West and Islamic world.

The first known quasi-democratic country was the Roman Republic (500 to 27 BC). In that system, an electorate comprising of aristocracy and landowners elected Senators. These senators had the mandate to elect, a person, as the Council that was comparable to the role of President in contemporary times. The term of office of the Council was just one year. Geographically Western Europe was part of this Republic, and its inhabitants were considered barbarians by the Romans. But as their population grew, along with their contribution to the economy, these so-called barbarians demanded representation. A lower house was mandated comprised of representatives elected by these second-class citizens. The mandate of the lower house was limited to taxation, customs, trade, property, and other economic spheres. These representatives of the lower house, for much of the Roman Republic, did not have the right to get the elevated status of Senators. The executive did not rely on their support that undermined their political power. It produced frequent civil unrest and demand for more concessions.

Almost 700 years before the start of the renaissance in the West, Islam arrived on the horizon. Roman Empire was at that time in relative decline after its division into an Eastern, which was later called Byzantine, and Western Roman Empire, that bifurcated into nation-states of France, Germany, Spain, Austria, etc. that we recognize today. Islam offered a social system in which each member of the community had a voice without reference to their land ownership, social or economic status. The Charter of Medina offered equal citizenship to all members of the community regardless of their religious affiliation (text of the charter of Medina provided in Appendix I). It was a new idea of egalitarianism that became one of the main building blocks of the vast expansion of the Islamic empire. It occurred during the first four rightly guided caliphs Abu Bakr (RATA), Omar (RATA), Uthman (RATA), and Ali (RATA). It was not just expansion in the geographic domain but also phenomenal growth in numbers of citizens because of the addition of conquered populations and new converts. The first civil unrest was the result of the demand for equal taxation and land rights from these new converts.

At the advent of renaissance, in the West, during the 14th to 17th centuries, new political systems emerged. These political institutions incorporated the voice of the people in the decisions of the community and the State. These transformations included the glorious revolution in England, the emergence of the French Republic after the revolution, the emergence of parliament in Prussia incorporating the Junker (landowner) class, and the democratic new world in especially the United States of America. But in these nascent democracies, the right to vote was limited to those that owned property or enjoyed a special citizenship status. It was not until the mid-1900s that the concept of universal adult franchise become a norm. The passage of the 19th amendment, in 1919, granted the women right to vote in United States of America.

After this brief history of the evolution of the adult franchise, the question remains, does the majority make the right decision for the community? When we look at the history of prophets and philosophers, it is clear, the majority do not always make the right decision. All prophets introduced a social change that was initially not acceptable to the majority and produced resistance. Similarly, in antiquity, when Greek philosopher Socrates started questioning the status quo, he was considered a danger to society, and a majority decided to punish him for that behavior. When Galileo presented the idea of earth revolving around the Sun, he was considered a political danger to society and banished from publishing his works. In our times, US President George W. Bush and British PM Tony Blair decided to invade Iraq based on lies, and the majority in these countries supported them for most of their tenure. One thing is clear that a nation starts its decline when majorities start making wrong decisions.

If it is possible that the majority can make a mistake, then what needs to change to put the community on the right track? Once again, we have to look at the lives of prophets and philosophers. They refused to accept the wrong decisions of the majority and go on preaching their message until a small group of followers emerged that firmly believed in the ideology and the social cause associated with it. From this nucleus of committed followers, it slowly starts expanding their network and converting their minority into a majority. The lesson is that reformation of a society is a long process and does not happen quickly. But throughout their struggle, they never engage in violence or forceful disruption of the community.

Bloody revolution to break the status quo for a short-term relief is a Western idea. An uprising of people that can become violent and disrupt life in a society is looked down upon by the Islamic political thought. It proposes a peaceful transformation of society that is evident from the life and tradition of Prophet Mohammad (PBUH).

Islamic political system does not give the absolute sovereign right to the majority but defines boundaries based on higher values within which the majority can draft regulations and laws. Islam proposes that when injustices happen in society, or the majority is finding itself helpless to challenge the forces of the oppressive status quo, then a group of people should start getting together to initiate a peaceful transformation. These people should first seek action from the officials of the State to redress the grievances. If they fail to deliver on their promises, then approach the justice system and demand prosecution of corrupt and unjust officials and community leaders. When these two options do not help, then they should start building a network throughout the nation to take political power away from the status quo. It is a peaceful process of transformation. The main component of it is to build a network of individuals that are capable and passionate about imposing the rule of justice and law in society. Transforming a nation is a long-term project. Sometimes it produces results after two or three generations.

Arab Spring in Middle Eastern countries, during the second decade of the 21st century, was an example of peaceful protests although they failed to achieve their political objectives in the short term. The main reasons for this failure were the lack of an underlying ideology, leadership, and political organization. But in the long term, these movements will inspire people to get together for a sustainable long-term change. All is not lost rather seed for future change is sown.

* * *

Recording History to Build a Nation

Humanity has to thank historians for its intellectual development from one generation to the other. Without this transfer of knowledge, a generation would have died with it rather than being able to transmit it to the next that then improves it further. The cycle repeats itself. The mode of this transmission were books, anecdotes, plays, and artisan skills. This recording of history is not limited to just social, cultural, and political aspects of our existence but also covers science and arts. When an artist paints a scene of a street, it transmits a lot of cultural information about the era.

It is next to impossible to completely record the history of an event and era without the introduction of distortions. These distortions are the result of the imperfection of our environment and flaws in the medium of communication. First, a moment of history is a collective essence of every single human being that has lived through it. Let me try to give an example. Let us suppose two Prime Ministers are meeting for a summit to discuss a geopolitical issue. At the entrance are two soldiers standing on guard duty. These soldiers will not be participating in the summit discussions, but we cannot say they are not affecting the history of that moment or outcome of the subsequent event. We cannot correctly predict how actions of insignificant actors of a historical event will have an impact on the overall outcome. Since a historian cannot be familiar with all these marginal stakeholders, it introduces a distortion in reporting of the whole event. In contemporary times there has been an effort to bring to light the histories of citizens of the era to have a holistic view of it. It is at an early stage of development.

The second hurdle in the recording of history is to know the exact motive of actors when they make decisions. A historian can only make a calculated judgment based on the outward expressions available in the form of speech, written statements, and subjective impressions of those that are present at the time. But this still cannot be considered the exact motive behind a historical event. Take, for example, the August 11th speech of founding father of Pakistan Mohammad Ali Jinnah or civil rights activist Martin Luther King 'I have a dream' speech. We can't say with certainty what was on their minds when they wrote these speeches, and because of that difficulty, there are various interpretations of it. Each ideological side wants to color the event to serve their biased agenda. Over time there could be many different interpretations of it. These distortions are augmented depending on the resources of the group that promotes it. Nazi Germany popularized their view of a superior race to inspire the nation to serve its expansionist agenda. All other points of view were relegated to the margins. Fundamentalist ideologies in East and West are also using a narrow view of history to gain popular mandate. It becomes hard to have an objective record of history.

The third hurdle in the recording of history is using language both as a transmitter and a communicating medium. It is not a static enterprise. It evolves. Some dialects have become extinct while the meaning of a word or a term change with time and does not remain the same. Similarly, new words and expressions are added to the language, while some words become extinct and are not in use any longer. To understand the full meaning of a significant political statement or agreement, the chronicler has to ensure that he knows the meanings associated with words or terms used at the time. It requires research in the development of language and the cultural influence on it. Even if historians learn the art of language, the difficulty remains that the reader has to have that same knowledge.

To overcome these three hurdles, philosophers and historians evolved methods that have to be employed to ensure the authenticity of a historical account. One thing is common in all these methodologies that the events are recorded or presented in a chronologically straight line. It starts with the oldest and moving towards the latest. In this approach, events are portrayed in sequence with the recording of dates, hierarchies, and relations. An event can be best understood by reading accounts of it by many historians from various perspectives before the hurdles mentioned above can be mitigated, to some extent.

The Quran, through numerous verses, validates recording of history as a learning tool for communities to progress and evolve.

Chapter 7 Verse 101: Such were the towns whosestoryWe (thus) relate unto thee: There came indeed to them their messengers with clear (signs): But they would not believe what they had rejected before. Thus doth Allah seal up the hearts of those who reject faith.

Chapter 12 Verse 3: We do relate unto thee the most beautiful of stories, in that We reveal to thee this (portion of the) Qur'an: before this, thou too was among those who knew it not.

Chapter 14 Verse 9: Has not thestoryreached you, (O people!), of those who (went) before you? - of the people of Noah, and 'Ad, and Thamud? - And of those who (came) after them? None knows them but Allah. To them came messengers with Clear (Signs); but they put their hands up to their mouths, and said: "We do deny (the mission) on which ye have been sent, and we are really in suspicious (disquieting) doubt as to that to which ye invite us."

Chapter 24 Verse 34: We have already sent down to you verses making things clear, an illustration from (thestoryof) people who passed away before you, and an admonition for those who fear (Allah).

Chapter 40 Verse 78: We did aforetime send messengers before thee: of them there are some whosestoryWe have related to thee, and some whosestoryWe have not related to thee. It was not (possible) for any messenger to bring a sign except by the leave of Allah: but when the Command of Allah issued, the matter was decided in truth and justice, and there perished, there and then those who stood on Falsehoods.

It recounts the stories of many past generations and experiences of Prophets. But there are certain salient features in the way Quran shares these histories. First, these events are not in chronological order. Surah Baqarah (Chapter # 2) talks about Prophet Musa (AS), he was the Prophet preceding Prophet Issa (AS) and Prophet Mohammad (PBUH) while other prophets appear much later. The second observation is that these stories do not shed any light on the cultural aspect of the times but remain focused on higher social and spiritual values presented by the events. The third observation is that there is hardly any genealogical information provided about the Prophets and other people mentioned in these stories. There is mention of father and son or husband and wife. It is different from the Bible or Ramayana that sometimes provides genealogical references up to 10 generations. It could mean that Quran suggests that although there is progress in scientific knowledge of humanity contributing towards the development of his consciousness of the reality of the natural world but the higher intellectual foundation, and the spiritual state has remained the same throughout the recorded history.

Another suggestion that the Quran makes is that despite repeated warnings and evidence that certain social conditions could be detrimental to society, humanity continues repeating these mistakes. One such example is charging interest that has been a source of many economic crises. Even Greek philosopher Aristotle labeled it as a social ill. Recent economic meltdown experienced by West and Southeast Asia can also be traced to leveraging which uses low interest borrowed capital to artificially inflate assets.

One impediment to the progress of any nation is its inability to record history with as much truthfulness and facts as possible. For instance, Pakistanis, of which I am a proud member, are still confused about whether they belong to South Asia or the Middle East/Central Asia. South Asian region is predominantly Hindu religiously different and culturally closer to her. Central Asia/Middle East which is religiously similar to her but culturally much different. The Quran validates the diversity of cultures, but we refuse to accept this allowance to our benefit and want to distort our cultural affiliation with South Asia to satisfy our religious zeal. This confusion is the result of misinterpreting history to create the perception of Pakistan aligned with Central Asia and the Middle East. Historians call such conditions torn countries. Pakistan is also torn geographically; Punjab and Sindh provinces are firmly culturally anchored with South Asia while Khyber Pakhtunkhwa and Baluchistan provinces find affinity towards Central Asia. A torn country cannot find stable ground to stand on and progress. Pakistani school's history syllabus has misleading information about past historical events. It projects false heroes, while real heroes are still looking for recognition. In such a situation, a nation cannot expect to progress when there is no solid foundation to inspire it. The first step towards stability will be to find an ideological anchor.

History is the trust historians can leave for the next generation to build on, and its absence produces a trust deficit and lack of self-confidence.

* * *

Share your thoughts: Did you like this book? Would you recommend it to others? Please share your candid review at your favorite platform Amazon, Barnes & Nobel, Kobo, Google Play or Apple Books.

Appendix I

Charter of Medinah
622 CE

In the name of God, the Compassionate, the Merciful.

(1) This is a document from Muhammad the prophet (governing the relations) between the believers and Muslims of Quraysh and Yathrib, and those who followed them and joined them and labored with them.

(2) They are one community (umma) to the exclusion of all men.

(3) The Quraysh emigrants according to their present custom shall pay the bloodwit within their number and shall redeem their prisoners with the kindness and justice common among believers.

(4-8) The B. 'Auf according to their present custom shall pay the bloodwit they paid in heatheism; every section shall redeem its prisoners with the kindness and justice common among believers. The B. Sa ida, the B. 'l-Harith, and the B. Jusham, and the B. al-Najjar likewise.

(9-11) The B. 'Amr b. 'Auf, the B. al-Nabit and the B. al-'Aus likewise.

(12)(a) Believers shall not leave anyone destitute among them by not paying his redemption money or bloodwit in kindness.

(12)(b) A believer shall not take as an ally the freedman of another Muslim against him.

(13) The God-fearing believers shall be against the rebellious or him who seeks to spread injustice, or sin or animosity, or corruption between believers; the hand of every man shall be against him even if he be a son of one of them.

(14) A believer shall not slay a believer for the sake of an unbeliever, nor shall he aid an unbeliever against a believer.

(15) God's protection is one, the least of them may give protection to a stranger on their behalf. Believers are friends one to the other to the exclusion of outsiders.

(16) To the Jew who follows us belong help and equality. He shall not be wronged, nor shall his enemies be aided.

(17) The peace of the believers is indivisible. No separate peace shall be made when believers are fighting in the way of God. Conditions must be fair and equitable to all.

(18) In every foray a rider must take another behind him.

(19) The believers must avenge the blood of one another shed in the way of God.

(20)(a) The God-fearing believers enjoy the best and most upright guidance.

(20)(b) No polytheist shall take the property of person of Quraysh under his protection, nor shall he intervene against a believer.

(21) Whoever is convicted of killing a believer without good reason shall be subject to retaliation unless the next of kin is satisfied (with blood-money), and the believers shall be against him as one man, and they are bound to take action against him.

(22) It shall not be lawful to a believer who holds by what is in this document and believes in God and the last day to help an evil-doer or to shelter him. The curse of God and His anger on the day of resurrection will be upon him if he does, and neither repentance nor ransom will be received from him.

(23) Whenever you differ about a matter it must be referred to God and to Muhammad.

(24) The Jews shall contribute to the cost of war so long as they are fighting alongside the believers.

(25) The Jews of the B. 'Auf are one community with the believers (the Jews have their religion and the Muslims have theirs), their freedmen and their persons except those who behave unjustly and sinfully, for they hurt but themselves and their families.

(26-35) The same applies to the Jews of the B. al-Najjar, B. al-Harith, B. Sai ida, B. Jusham, B. al-Aus, B. Tha'laba, and the Jafna, a clan of the Tha'laba and the B. al-Shutayba. Loyalty is a protection against treachery. The freedmen of Tha 'laba are as themselves. The close friends of the Jews are as themselves.

(36) None of them shall go out to war save the permission of Muhammad, but he shall not be prevented from taking revenge for a wound. He who slays a man without warning slays himself and his household, unless it be one who has wronged him, for God will accept that.

(37) The Jews must bear their expenses and the Muslims their expenses. Each must help the other against anyone who attacks the people of this document. They must seek mutual advice and consultation, and loyalty is a protection against treachery. A man is not liable for his ally's misdeeds. The wronged must be helped.

(38) The Jews must pay with the believers so long as war lasts.

(39) Yathrib shall be a sanctuary for the people of this document.

(40) A stranger under protection shall be as his host doing no harm and committing no crime.

(41) A woman shall only be given protection with the consent of her family.

(42) If any dispute or controversy likely to cause trouble should arise it must be referred to God and to Muhammad the apostle of God. God accepts what is nearest to piety and goodness in this document.

(43) Quraysh and their helpers shall not be given protection.

(44) The contracting parties are bound to help one another against any attack on Yathrib.

(45)(a) If they are called to make peace and maintain it they must do so; and if they make a similar demand on the Muslims, it must be carried out except in the case of a holy war.

(45)(b) Everyone shall have his portion from the side to which he belongs.

(46) The Jews of al-Aus, their freedmen and themselves have the same standing with the people of this document in purely loyalty from the people of this document. Loyalty is a protection against treachery. He who acquires ought to acquire it for himself. God approves of this document.

(47) This deed will not protect the unjust and the sinner. The man who goes forth to fight and the man who stays at home in the city is safe unless he has been unjust and sinned. God is the protector of the good and God-fearing man and Muhammad is the apostle of God.

References

Books

- Ali, Abdullah Yusuf, *The Holy Qur'an (translation)*, Wordworth Editions Ltd, ISBN: 978-1853267826
- Dawkins, Richard, *The God Delusion*, Mariner Books, ISBN: 978-0618918249
- Descartes, Rene, *Meditations on First Philosophy*, Hackett Publishing Company, ISBN: 978-0872201927
- Freud, Sigmund, *Dream Psychology*, The James A. McCann Company, Public Domain book
- *Holy Bible, King James Version*, Christian Art Publishers, ISBN: 978-1432102401
- Jung, Carl G., *The theory of Psychoanalysis*, The Journal of Nervous and Mental Disease Publishing Company, Public domain book
- McCauley, Robert N., *Why Religion is Important and Science is not*, Oxford University Press, ISBN: 978-0199827268
- Russell, Bertrand, *History of Western Philosophy*, Simon & Schuster/Touchstone, ISBN: 978-0671201586
- Walker, Matthew, *Why We Sleep: Unlocking the power of sleep and dreams*, Simon & Schuster, ISBN: 978-1501144325

* * *

Videos

- Allan Watts Interview Bertrand Russell: https://www.youtube.com/playlist?list=PL6C2F2A96708F26F9
- Bertrand Russell – Face to Face interview (BBC, 1959): https://www.youtube.com/watch?v=1bZv3pSaLtY Or https://youtu.be/wxpaC7pi5Ko
- Inside Animal Minds – Bird Genius: https://www.youtube.com/watch?v=-spBaywak7M
- Inside Animal Minds – Who is the smartest? https://www.youtube.com/watch?v=B5DTOWnFSCs
- Inside Animal Minds – Dogs and super senses: https://www.youtube.com/watch?v=rY5AtyvjPWQ
- The purpose of life – a presentation by Prof. Jeffery Lang: https://www.youtube.com/watch?v=wjnTngSxlXo

* * *

Wikipedia and Web Links

- Einstein and theory of relativity: https://en.wikipedia.org/wiki/Theory_of_relativity
- Mansur al Hallaj: https://en.wikipedia.org/wiki/Mansur_Al-Hallaj
- Roman Empire: https://en.wikipedia.org/wiki/Roman_Empire
- Religion: https://www.bbc.com/future/article/20141219-will-religion-ever-disappear
- Jesus Lost Years: https://en.wikipedia.org/wiki/Unknown_years_of_Jesus

About the Author

Abdul Quayyum Khan Kundi is known for his contributions to Pakistani newspapers through op-ed columns. He has shared his insights on a wide range of topics including politics, social issues, and foreign policy. His writing has appeared in prominent publications such as Independent Urdu, The Daily Times, The Frontier Post, and Pakistan Today.

In a particular op-ed column dated December 14, 2011, Mr. Kundi discussed the emergence of a new multi-polar world order. He argued that American hegemony was being challenged by a collaborative effort between China and Russia, leading to the development of a new cold war scenario. This topic reflects his engagement with global geopolitics and international relations.

Mr. Kundi has also authored several books that delve into various subjects. His first book, "Freedom by Choice," is a compilation of writings that explore US-Pakistan relations, reforms in the Muslim world, and the balance of power in South Asia. This book showcases his keen interest in diplomacy and regional dynamics.

"Lessons from the Quran," his second book, focuses on Quranic verses with an emphasis on their relevance to social values. This work highlights his engagement with religious and ethical matters.

His book titled "Islamic Social Contract" is a significant effort to propose a political system rooted in the social values outlined in the Quran and the Sunnah (tradition) of the Prophet Mohammad (PBUH). Mr. Kundi believes that the Muslim world's political liberation can only be achieved by developing systems that align with Islamic cultural traditions. This book offers a framework for building stable societies, drawing from the context of reform movements like the "Arab Spring."

Finally, his book "Thoughts" is a collection of metaphysical speculations covering topics related to religion, philosophy, and science. This work reflects his intellectual curiosity and willingness to explore abstract and philosophical ideas.

In summary, Abdul Quayyum Khan Kundi is a multifaceted thinker and writer who has made contributions to the discussion of politics, religion, and global affairs, particularly within the context of Pakistan and the Muslim world.

You can connect with me on:

- http://abdulqkundi.com
- https://twitter.com/aqkkundi
- http://facenook.com/abdul.quayyum.khan.kundi

Also by Abdul Quayyum Khan Kundi

Islamic Social Contract

Islamic Social Contract" ventures beyond being merely a religious doctrine, aiming to present a comprehensive way of life. Rooted in the Quran and the teachings of Prophet Mohammad (PBUH), this book endeavors to construct a political framework derived from these foundational sources. It represents a proposal for the Muslim majority to contemplate and potentially embrace an alternative to the prevalent Western secular democracy.

In offering an Islamic constitution, the book tackles certain deficiencies within the Western model. It strives to address these gaps by integrating principles from Islamic teachings, thereby presenting an alternative political structure that draws from the inherent strengths and values of the Islamic tradition.